# When the *Dream* is **BIG** Enough

*The Journey of a Professional Networker*

Johnna Parr

# When the *Dream* is **BIG** Enough

## *The Journey of a Professional Networker*

978-0-578-01458-6

We invite you to visit the author at:

www.whenthedreamisbigenough.com

or

johnna@mjparr.com

*Given to:*

_____

*From:*

_____

*Date:*

_____

*Because YOU are believed in!*

This book is dedicated to you.

I believe everything we experience in life has a purpose.

There is a reason you are holding this book
in your hands.

Make it yours. Use a highlighter, mark it up and learn.

I am thankful to all of the business leaders, authors and
teachers that helped shape my learning experience. I thank
God and I am honored that you are allowing me to assist
in shaping yours.

It is my biggest desire that the information from this book
will influence and inspire you, change your life forever,

and make you realize that

ANYTHING is possible

When the

# When the *Dream* is **BIG** Enough

# Table of Contents

# Foreword

# Everything Happens
# for a Reason

*Sometimes God has to thump you on the head, literally,
to get your attention.*

Since 1998, I have had the honor to speak to and
teach – from individuals in their living rooms to crowds
of several thousand. I have evolved into a leader and have
become a millionaire in an industry that allows anyone to
start with nothing but a dream, and become financially
free. I have a passion and love for this business, and have
shared that passion around the country. I kept all of the
journals, speeches and teachings I had written over the
last decade. I knew that someday I would use those notes
for a good purpose.

Today is that day.

Several weeks ago, I had an accident. I felt light-
headed while in the powder room off our family room. I
stood up and called for my husband, Matt. The next thing

that I remember is waking up on the floor, blood flowing down my throat and looking up at Matt; who had a look on his face that I had never seen before – fear. He was holding me and screaming for me to breathe. He then frantically dialed 911; telling the operator that his wife had hit her head and had a seizure.

Several days in the intensive care unit and every test under the sun led the medical professionals to the conclusion that I fainted; the fainting caused me to free fall and hit my head on the floor; the intensity of the head injury led to the seizure.

This made me feel slightly better because the biggest issue was, "did the seizure cause the fall or did the fall cause the seizure?" Kind of, like, what came first – the chicken or the egg? The fact that the head trauma caused the seizure seemed a little better; however, a seizure is a seizure. The prognosis was no driving or traveling for 90 days. I was "grounded". The neurologist also told Matt, because of the head injury, "NO stress, only rest and relaxation". So, Matt made an executive decision: he put me on a temporary leave of absence from any business activity for 90 days. He wanted me to focus on my healing, inside and out.

I have always heard the phrase, it hurts to heal. The healing has been challenging and frustrating at times with debilitating headaches, being painfully sensitive to light, and having challenges with blurred vision, focusing and the ability to read.

Being out of the loop for three months in any other career or business would absolutely cripple an individual and threaten their income. Our network marketing business continued to flourish and grow.

Cancelling my travel schedule made me realize how fortunate we are to be able to travel and vacation as we do. I cancelled a trip to the East Coast, West Coast, a Caribbean cruise, a trip to Louisiana, a charity motorcycle event in Fort Lauderdale, Florida, the grand opening of a leaders retreat , and a 12-day private villa vacation in the Turks and Caicos Islands. Wow, how blessed we are! We are blessed with absolute freedom – a lifestyle that is only possible with free time and money.

Initially, being "grounded" felt like a life sentence; I would miss several events, vacations and seeing dear friends around the country. However, I then started to feel comfortable in the sabbatical and realized that "everything happens for a reason". Our job is to look for the seed of opportunity in every adversity or challenge, and ask ourselves, "What can I learn from this experience?" "How can I use this to further serve others?" Every challenge or upsetting situation can become a teacher. In life, we have many teachers and, with every experience, we have the opportunity to grow and evolve.

I viewed every good day as a victory and one step closer to being 100%. It was on these good days that I began to write and review the papers that I had written over the last decade. I revisited the times when I was first starting out, reliving the journey as we progressed through the different levels of achievement, the trials and tribulations that led to our victories, the struggles that led to the prize and, most importantly, the mistakes we made, and the valuable lessons that we learned, along the way.

One thing I do know for sure: from first-hand experience, even when you do fall flat on your face, you are still moving forward.

As I was recovering, the words that played over and over in my head were "BE still and know that I AM God". (Psalm 46:10) It invites us to be silent, mindful and in prayer. I am relishing the stillness and I am honored to be able to share with you.

### *Erma Bombeck wrote:*

*"When I stand before God at the end of my life, I would hope that I would have not a single bit of talent left and could say,*

*'I used everything YOU gave me'."*

Johnna

# Chapter 1

# A Day in the Life

**I entered network marketing as a single mom of two daughters, ages 2 and 4.** I began to imagine what my life could become. I learned to become a student, and then became a teacher and then evolved into a leader. I admired and respected the man who introduced me to the business. Over the years he became my business mentor and one of my dearest friends. That friendship turned into a deep love for each other and we were married in January of 1999.

We have built a successful network marketing business for over a decade. Today, our business continues to grow and increase, even though our time in the business doesn't grow or increase. We build this business around our life, around our children, around the things we love to do.

It has meant FREEDOM, an abundance of time with an abundance of money. *Webster* defines FREEDOM as: the absence of constraint in choice or action, liberation from restraint, from the power of another, the power to choose what one does.

## Do you want a *normal* life?

Normal is double-income families. Normal is children being raised by someone other than a parent. Normal is substantial credit card debt. Normal is rarely taking a vacation. Normal is not having a savings account. Normal is living paycheck to paycheck. Normal is debt going up, and income staying the same. Normal is limited time with family and friends. Normal is not having the time to do the things we really love to do. Normal is just getting by. Normal is having no control of your income. Normal is feeling out of control.

I am so thankful that this wonderful industry entered my life because today, I can proudly say, that I am completely ABNORMAL!

It is abnormal to take one vacation a month. It is abnormal to take several international vacations a year. It is abnormal to have no credit card debt. It is abnormal to have your possessions paid for. It is abnormal to have a healthy savings account and investments. It is abnormal to be able to give abundantly to charity, churches and missions around the world. It is abnormal to have substantial time together as a family. It is abnormal to have control over your financial future and destiny. It is abnormal to have total FREEDOM.

## A Day in the Life

It is abnormal to be able to decide what YOU want to do each day of your life. I love being ABNORMAL! A wise man said, "See what the masses are doing, and go the opposite way." Matt and I chose to run the opposite way.

The real freedom of our business is not felt in all of the vacations that we take, although that is part of it. It is felt in our daily life and in our daily experiences.

In the earlier years of building our business, I had an experience while taking Monica, our youngest daughter, to kindergarten. I walked her inside and was greeted in the doorway of the classroom by one of her friends. When I looked at him, his eyes were puffy, his nose was red and he was coughing. As I walked back to my car, I felt anger at his mother, "how could his mother bring him to school in this condition? Doesn't she realize he is sick and should be in bed?" I then abruptly stopped myself, shook it off, and realized, she probably doesn't have a choice. How much time can she take off of work? How many sick or vacation days has she already taken?

The very next day, Monica woke up coughing and sneezing. I didn't have a challenge or a problem; I didn't have to call anyone at work to make an excuse. I simply tucked her back in bed and said, "Stay in bed, honey, you don't have to go anywhere, Mommy is home." I was very thankful to have the option that no other career or traditional business can offer.

We have breakfast together as a family. The only ones rushing out the door are our daughters going off to school. One particular morning I remember being so thankful that we had this time together. It was the beginning of the school year, and I had fresh flowers around our home. Monica was about to enter second grade so she asked me if she could bring some of the flowers to her new teacher. I thought this was very sweet of her, so we choose the most beautiful flowers from several of the vases, tied them with string and made a bouquet. I asked Sabrina, who was entering the fourth grade, "Would you like to bring a bouquet to your teacher?" She shrugged her shoulders, made a scrunched-up face and said, "I think I am going to wait a couple of days." "Why?" I asked. She looked at me and looked at Matt and exclaimed, "I am not sure she deserves them yet." With that, Matt almost fell out of his chair and hooped his coffee all at the same time.

That afternoon, Sabrina came running into the house excitedly saying, "I am definitely bringing flowers to my teacher tomorrow!" Monica, dragging behind her, looked up to me in disgust, "I shouldn't have brought her any."

Now, I know this story is a simple story describing a typical day in the life of a family. *But, is it really?* If I would have gone back into corporate America, instead of building my network marketing business, I would have missed *all* of it. I may have been there in the morning,

4

but I would have been busy making sure that my needs were met because I would have been rushing out the door with the children, or maybe before. I definitely would have missed them coming off the bus that afternoon.

For most people, they have to fit their life in around their income-producing activities, whether that income-producing activity is a job or traditional business. They have so many weeks' vacation, so many sick days, they go to work at the same time, have lunch around the same time, and arrive home around the same time. They have to fit their life around their job or business.

***When you succeed in network marketing, your income will revolve around your life.***

You are able to *live* your life, and put all of the people you love *first*, and all of the things that you love to do *first*, and all of the places that you want to go *first*, and you can fit your network marketing business in around those people, places, things and experiences.

Someone had asked me to document a typical day in our life. I decided to document a simple, middle of the week Wednesday.

7:00 a.m. – Alarm goes off. I wake up and before my feet hit the floor I say a prayer of thanks for all of the blessings that are in our life.

7:30 a.m. – I wake up the girls and tell both of them, "It is going to be a great day today!" This is our daily mantra.

7:45 a.m. – I go down into the kitchen and make lunches and breakfast.

8:00 a.m. – I wake up Matt and we all have breakfast together.

8:45 a.m. – The girls are off to school. Matt and I check into our home office. We review or planners, our goals and mission statements, check email.

9:00 a.m. – Matt and I listen to a business development conference call.

9:45 a.m. – We hit our fitness center, work out and take a steam.

11:00 a.m. – The housekeepers arrive.

11:15 a.m. – It is a beautiful day! Matt fills all of the bird feeders in the back. Our home is adjacent to 10,000 acres of preserved forest land so the wildlife is abundant. We sit on the back deck and read for a while.

12:00 noon – I go inside and prepare lunch. We dine alfresco, enjoying this sunny day.

2:00 p.m. – Matt leaves for a meeting with a business owner he met on an airplane last week. The business owner is excited to see our network marketing business because he is looking to diversify his income.

3:00 p.m. – Girls come home from school. I am waiting for them at the kitchen island, opening mail. We have a snack, visit and talk about their day. Being that they are teenagers, I am so thankful that I am home at this time of the day. They then go upstairs and do their homework in the library.

3:30 p.m. – Matt arrives home from a successful meeting.

6:00 p.m. – Dinner together, we choose our dinner time and fit our business in around it. Dinner time is our time to "fix and celebrate". We talk about our challenges and our victories that day.

7:00 p.m. – Matt and I have a busy night on the phone. Matt goes into our home office. I go into the Red Room and start a fire in the fireplace. We spend the next couple of hours fielding phone calls, closing meetings for our team across the country.

7:00 p.m. – In the meantime, Sabrina and Monica are on their own schedule. During this busy time, Sabrina practises her guitar, Monica plays the piano.

9:00 p.m. – Talk with the girls before bed, prayers, and kiss goodnight.

10:00 p.m. – We pop popcorn, watch a movie.

When I reviewed what I had documented on this day, a Wednesday, I realized how truly grateful I was that that network marketing came into my life. I am thankful that I didn't take the opportunity for granted.

We now have the ability to design our life EVERY DAY and fit our business in around it. EVERY DAY is different. EVERY DAY is special, and EVERY DAY is a gift.

Even though this day was uneventful, it was awesome in the fact that we decided WHAT we were going to do, WHEN we were going to do it, and with WHOM we would spend it.

## If you were to design a perfect day, what would it look like?

## You too can design your life, as we do ours….**EVERY** DAY.

# Chapter 2

# Network Marketing, The Industry that Works

**Today, I embrace an industry that many have laughed or sneered at, and swore they would never touch – network marketing**. "Network Marketing" can also be called "Direct Selling". It dates back as early as 2000 B.C. Today, according to recent surveys, 55% of all Americans have purchased goods or services through this industry. The industry has grown 90% in the last decade and sales in the United States are more than $30 billion annually. Neil Offen, the President of the Direct Selling Association is quoted as saying, "I congratulate all of you on this industry-wide achievement. All of you are keeping the American Dream, being one's boss and directly relating effort to reward, alive and well in our country."

*Fortune* magazine states that, "The modern world is on the verge of another leap in creativity and productivity but the job is not going to be a part of tomorrow's economic reality."

# When the Dream is Big Enough

Robert Kiyosaki, the worldwide best-selling author and financial educator says, "A network marketing business is a new and revolutionary way to achieve wealth. The network marketing industry continues to grow faster than franchises or traditional business."

I feel the greatest form of free enterprise is network marketing. No other industry offers everyone the opportunity to start with nothing but a dream and become financially free! It treats everyone the same.

If our travels around the world have taught us anything, it is we are so blessed to be living in the United States of America. Most envy the opportunities we enjoy, and many would give up their families, their friends and their material possessions just to live in a country with unlimited opportunities. Yet, even living in this country of freedom, many are living in occupational slavery: their lifestyle, their hours, their working conditions, vacations and other conditions are dictated and determined by someone else.

***If you are working for someone else,
you are building someone else's dream.***

Many traditional business owners, who have that wonderful entrepreneurial spirit, are often disheartened because being a small business owner means long hours, headaches and, in the long run, their business winds up owning them – they have limited free time.

For most people, when they stop working, their income stops.

There is no traditional job, career or small business that offers both time and money. A network marketing business does. It is a business model that provides equal opportunity to all people, regardless of age, gender, background, nationality or religion. Anyone can further their own well-being through personal effort and initiative. It is an opportunity that is not limited to those who have special skills, education, financial status or large amounts of capital to invest. It treats everyone equally!

Each person is allowed the freedom to decide the amount of time, energy and commitment they are willing to put into it. You will learn that the best way to build the business is to serve others. One of our favorite sayings is, *"I must serve my team so that I may lead."*

You will learn how to evaluate qualities in people early on, qualities such as passion, willingness to learn and ability. You will look at family and friends differently, and will be amazed that some may not be as supportive as you would have hoped.

You will be challenged to look inward at yourself, you will be forced to look in the mirror, you will have to take responsibility for your actions, or lack of action. You may not like what you see at first, but you can make the changes necessary to become victorious.

A network marketing business is not for wishers, whiners, waiters or watchers. It is not for those who have no ambition and choose to sit home and watch television every night. It is not for those who are content with the status quo.

This is a business that is for doers and dreamers, for those who are never content with average. This is a business for those who are successful, yet dissatisfied. It is a business for those who are looking for the right path to their highest dreams.

**_I am a dreamer, a BIG dreamer, and I am proud of it._**

As you begin on your journey, you will realize that this business is about confronting ourselves, and confronting our fears and seeing how we stack up in the world. There are excellent recognition systems and pay scales that let us know that we can *do* more and, *if* we do more, we can *have* more and *become* more. If we don't move up the ranks, it is not only obvious to us; it is obvious to those around us. It holds us accountable. When we see others move up, it gives us hope, "if they can do it, so can I".

Praise and recognition are the most powerful forms of motivation. Nothing encourages people to work harder and produce quality results like having their accomplishments noticed and praised.

One thing I do not understand in our society is where and to whom the recognition goes to. Average behavior is condoned, corruption and crime is eulogized, athletes and entertainers are uplifted to superstar status, giving them influence over our society, when the real heroes – the police officers, firefighters, doctors, nurses, teachers, ministers and our American soldiers – get virtually no recognition.

What I love about network marketing is that it singles people out, people like you and me, and acknowledges us and recognizes us when we do something great. When you serve others and help them become successful, and you do this with *integrity*, with *character* and with *values*, YOU will be recognized and you will get paid beyond your wildest dreams. Anyone can be a hero in this arena. *It is the only true arena where we can test ourselves against negative influences and win again and again and again.*

A network is made up of people you know and will meet, and the people they know and meet, and the people they know and meet. What is tremendous about the dynamic growth of a network is its endless possibilities. When you make a list of those that you know, it doesn't end there. You don't know who they know, and who they know, and who they know.

*Anyone can cut open an apple and count the seeds, but no one can tell how many apples will come from just one seed.*

Your goal is to sift and sort to find those that want what you have. You are looking for lookers.

As you begin your sifting and sorting process, you will come across essentially three different types of people with three different predispositions. Predisposition means that their opinions are already there and in place before you even picked up the phone to call.

The first are those that have a prejudicial view. *Webster* defines prejudice as follows:

"**¹prej·u·dice (1):** preconceived judgment or opinion **(2):** an adverse opinion or leaning formed without just grounds or before sufficient knowledge b: an instance of such judgment or opinion c: an irrational attitude of hostility directed against an individual, a group, a race, or their supposed characteristics."

These are those people that have already made their mind up before you ever contacted them. They have an incorrect assumption about the industry of network marketing, and they are not open to hearing *any* information. They are completely closed-minded. This has *nothing* to do with you; it has *everything* to do with their prejudiced view.

The second are those that are skeptical. They aren't completely closed-minded. This is the group that will need extra testimonials and belief builders before they make any type of decision. I welcome skepticism if the prospect is willing to meet halfway and honestly wants more information before making a decision. Skepticism is good; cynicism is something I can't help with.

The third are those that are open-minded, those that have not decided one way or another. These are the prospects that are easily led through the process. They are open and their timing is NOW.

The key is to sort through the first two groups to find the third group.

*A very important phrase for me was:*
*Amateurs convince and professionals sort.*

I wanted to be a professional and get paid for my efforts. Convincing was too tiring and fruitless. If I had to convince someone to get into business with me, I had to then convince this person to work the business. I could have spent that time more wisely finding someone who had the desire in the first place.

Remember, no matter what business you choose, there will always be the doomsayers and the naysayers, who will tell you it won't work.

*Those too weak to go after their own dreams*
*will always find a way to discourage others.*

In order to get to the freedom that you want in your life, you have to become an *over-comer*. And in order to overcome, you have to extinguish the fear. It is about stepping out in faith. It is living as if it already is. Faith and fear *will not* and *cannot* co-exist. Where there is fear, there is no faith. How could I possibly build the life I wanted to live, if *I* doubted and didn't believe?

I remember staring at the list of names, questioning. I remember feeling my voice and hands shake as I made my first calls. I remember fearing what someone would say. I told Matt I was scared, he simply looked at me and said, "Do it afraid! Just do it afraid." As Teddy Roosevelt said, "Do the thing you fear the most, and the death of fear is certain."

**When your belief in YOU and YOUR DREAM**
**is greater than your belief in other people's opinions,**
**You will have mastered your life.**

People have opinions about everything. There have been many opinions about different things over the years; here is an example of some people's opinions about a very familiar industry. "In most American's minds, it's a scam and a scheme, questionable or unethical at best." And another opinion, "Many own your own business entrepreneurial hopefuls have been hyped into turning over their life savings, only to see the company go out of business, and take their dreams down with them."

The funny thing about the above opinions is that they were written about franchising in the 1960s. All of those negative feelings and opinions were being said about an industry which today is responsible for more than 40% of all the retail goods and services in the United States alone, over $1 trillion. Franchising started to earn acceptance because you could no longer ignore the results; with acceptance came more positive results.

*Never forget that people tend to reject things that they simply do not understand.*

The network marketing industry is beginning to receive mainstream recognition. Billionaire Donald Trump has written in high regards to its merit. Robert Kiyosaki has written books about it, and has said, "Many people ask me if it is a pyramid. I simply say that a corporation is really a pyramid, one person at the top, and everyone below. A successful network marketing business is the exact opposite. A network marketing company doesn't succeed unless it brings its people to the top."

This is a business based on, "What can I do for you?" not, "What can you do for me?" Your organization or team does not work for you, you are not their boss: *you* work for them. If you want to create wealth, keep the attitude of "I work for you. What do you need? How can I help you?" Your team is not working hard to get you to *your* goals. They are working hard to get to *their goals.*

## Mastering the art of duplication

The most important element to *explosive growth* and *residual income* is **duplication**. Many believe that when they bring on a business partner, they have duplicated themselves. Actually the full cycle of duplication is:

You bring on a business partner, you teach them to bring on a business partner, and they teach them to bring on a business partner.

It is a Biblical principal, "Each one reach one and teach one to reach one." We call it "teaching the teachers to teach the teachers to teach".To accomplish this, it is vital to teach the process to your new business partners in the simplest fashion. Teach them in a form that would be easily duplicable. You don't just want to teach someone how to build a big and profitable business; you want to teach them *how* to teach it to someone else.

The key to dynamic growth and team building is a **uniform business system.** Uniformity is highly important so that growth can continue through many levels within your organization. If one leader does the business one way, then teaches another. the person that they are teaching will put their own spin on the process, and try it another way; then their person will go another route. This causes confusion in the team. A confused team is a paralyzed team and no action will be taken.

If everyone is teaching the same process, everyone can take part in the process, and growth will be substantial and long term. Your team should have a constant and, more importantly, consistent source of reference.

### *The mother of ALL learning is repetition.*

Repetition is the key to learning, so repeating the same processes is the key to teaching. Once the process is learned, let your people take ownership of their business.

The uniform system should be in many forms because people receive information differently. A written manual is vital for reference and important for business scripts; audios, DVDs and web files are essential.

### Four things that MUST be done

**1. Remove any distractions**. *Temporary inconvenience for a lifetime of convenience.* You may have to, in the beginning, set aside certain hobbies or extra-curricular activities, while you are building the foundation of your business. Once the foundation is in place, the activity of that foundation will take over. The income of the business will not only be from your effort, it will be derived from the activity and volume production of your entire team. You have to be willing to take time *now* to build your future.

Some things may have to be set aside for a short while; but understand, the things that you put off for a short while now you will be able to do *as often* and *as much* as you like *later.*

When you succeed with your network marketing business, your business will revolve around your life. Your life comes first; the things you love to do, the people you want to be with, the places you want to go will come first, and you can fit your business around your life. In order to get *there*, you MUST remove the distractions and non-income producing activities for a short while.

When Matt and I married, he saw how long it took me to clean the house. He calculated how much money we could make if I dedicated that same amount of time building our business, making calls and assisting the team. We were actually losing money. The extra business income, that week, would more than pay for a housekeeper.

Hire a neighborhood kid to mow the lawn or plow your driveway. You can't create wealth doing those activities. I had a conversation with a leader in regards to cutting the lawn. I asked him how much it would cost to hire someone to do that same job. He answered about $10.00 per hour. I then said, "When *you* are cutting your lawn; that is how much *you* are worth, $10.00 per hour, not a penny more. If you spent that same time building your business, your time could be worth millions of dollars in the future." He hired someone the very next day.

We realized, early on, that if we kept our network marketing business on the back burner and we kept saying "tomorrow I will do it" it would NEVER be successful. If we treated it like a hobby, it would pay like a hobby.

We have a sign in our office that says "Freedom, some sacrifice required". Because of the short-term sacrifices that we made along the way, today we have all of the time to enjoy all of the things we wish to do, and we have the money to do them.

**2. Remember WHY you are doing this.** Don't get caught up with the negatives. Focus on what you want and claim it every day. Matt and I read a written statement every morning and every evening. Design and describe what you want your life to look like, mentally, emotionally, spiritually, financially, physically, and make it already present for you. Get excited about it. This is YOUR life! If you focus on your reasons WHY, this creates an emotional juice that keeps you going when the going gets tough. Keep your eyes on the prize, and *enjoy* the process. Don't view the process as a struggle, enjoy the moment, and know that every little thing that you are doing, no matter how great or how small, every step, every call, every meeting is taking you closer to your dream.

Develop a goal board, a dream board, a vision board. It doesn't matter what you call it, just do it. There is a tremendous power in visualization. Cut out pictures of things, and also include powerful statements and put them on a board and look at the board each day. While you are looking at the pictures, envision your life and believe that those things are already present for you in your life. "How does this make you *feel?*" This powerful feeling and emotion is a very important part of the process. Tap into this emotion daily.

**3. Remain encouraged**. The biggest killer of dreams is discouragement. One thing that all winners have in common is *how* they handle discouragement.

*10% of life happens,*
*90% of life is how we react to what happens.*

Most think that those of us that are successful have fewer problems or lesser challenges than others. The fact is; we have had *more*, which is *why* we are successful. We have had *more* people tell us "no", *more* people tell us that this wouldn't work, more people no show us for meetings than *you*. We just kept going! We kept our eyes on the prize and *we stopped stopping*.

Some of you are already in the process of building your business, and some of the people that make up your business team are not moving as fast as you would like. Love them where they are at and *stop waiting* on them. Go find those who *want* it. Don't do it *for* them, do it *with* them and build a team of leaders that *want* to build a *productive* and *profitable* business.

***Keep looking. Nothing will ignite your fire more than to bring on a new business partner that has desire, work ethic and a big dream.***

One of the most important things for me was to read books that would add value to my life. Something that would keep my head on track, something positive that would offset a negative world. Your team is looking to you for inspiration and encouragement. You cannot give to them what you do not have. If your well is dry, how can you possibly quench the thirst of your team?

Who are you associating with? There are two people in this world, dream believers and dream stealers, people who lift you up or tear you down. Matt and I made a conscious decision to listen to the dream believers, those who believed in us and were cheering us on.

Discipline your disappointments. The rewards at the top are too great to let a few stubbed toes keep you from achieving your dreams.

**4. Rely upon the system.** You must ask yourself, "Is what I am doing easily duplicated?" I am often astounded that so many stray from the *proven* path into the ditch of failure. Good duplication equals residual income. Without good duplication there is no residual income.

When I reference "the system" I am referring to all of it. Not just the recruiting process. It is plugging your teammates into the whole process. They must feel a part of the bigger picture. If it is all about *you*, it will *always* be all about you. If you choose to be the omnipotent, all-powerful OZ, everything will stop in your absence. A fundamental principle is "You can give a man to fish and feed him for a day, or you can teach a man *how* to fish, and he will feed himself for a lifetime." Your job is to teach your organization to fish well, and teach them to develop their own successful businesses, which is part of your business.

If you become system reliant, in your absence the show will go on, but ONLY if you completely rely upon the entire system, and *teach* your team to do the same.

## All great network marketing companies have systems that do three very important things.

**1. Put them in.** The company should have a variety of business tools to provide information about the company's products and its services. It should also offer professional recruiting materials to aid in your recruitment of new business partners. They should be easy to use and cost effective. Some companies offer websites, printed materials, promotional videos, web links, conference calls and third-party documentation etc.

**2. Keep them in.** Keeping people plugged in and inspired is essential. Our goal is to keep people plugged in long enough until that person "gets it". Everyone starts with a different learning curve. Everyone starts with a different level of belief. Their level of belief in the company, the products or, most importantly, themselves, is the one determining factor in how effective this person will be at building their business. That is why we encourage reading books that will aid in personal development and attending meetings and events.

High quality products and services, conference calls, web links, up-line support, promotional and teaching materials, meetings, events and national conventions are extremely important to the belief-building process.

### *Those that believe will build.*

Events are the glue. Our goal was to always have a large group at the events because we knew the event was highly effective in keeping people fired up and re-engaged - being a part of something larger than them, and becoming part of the whole team, joining together in the greater cause. The people that attend the events are always light years ahead of those who don't.

**3. Move them along and up the ranks**. When good recognition programs are in place, your team will continually want to pursue the next level of achievement. This will give them additional income and stability to their business, which adds stability to yours. When *you* become recognized, you will motivate your team to achieve the same level. If you are stagnant, guess what, your team will become stagnant. *The recognition programs create a benchmark for action.*

The entire system creates unity and a climate for *growth.* You can always tell when someone is not plugged in. They are out of synch with the entire team. Instead of being an asset to the team, they tend to be a liability. They don't attend conference calls or training events; therefore they don't know the same information that the team knows. They tend to innovate instead of duplicate. Because of this, they will confuse other team members. In order for your business to run like a well-oiled machine, you have to do your best to keep your *entire* team plugged into the *entire* system.

Most don't get their team plugged in early enough. This is a vital step. When you bring on a new business partner, assist them in getting plugged in early on, introduce them to your up-line leadership, those people that have a vested interest in their success. Make an effort to keep your existing organization plugged in, and then teach them how to keep their organizations plugged in.

## The Timing is NOW

Have you noticed that there are some major changes happening in our country? We are in the information age. Network marketing is all about information, and sharing that information with others. It is an industry that will flourish during tough economic times because people are looking for options and additional streams of income: a network marketing business will be their answer.

There has never been a better time for the good people of our country to start making some serious money. You do know what the golden rule is? Yes, "Do unto others as you would have them do unto you" is one of them. The *other* golden rule is, "Those with the gold make the rules."

The moral fabric of any society is in the hands of those that have the money. Isn't it time we put the money in the hands of those that have values? Those that have integrity? Those that have character?

This is the only industry that can do just that, it joins all of us together. A mass of people going after their dreams by helping others achieve theirs. Is there anything more positive than that? This is an industry that brings people together in one accord in servant hood.

It gives everyone the same opportunities to have anything they want to have, become anything they want to be, to go anywhere they want to go, help anyone they want to help, and to give anything they want to give.

Do you want to make a difference? Do you want to effect positive change in the lives of others? Network marketing is the wave of the future and *is* the answer.

# Chapter 3

# When the Student is Ready, The Teacher Appears

**When I was first introduced to this industry, I attended several teaching events**. I kept hearing certain phrases.

"When the **student** is ready, the teacher appears."

"First you're the **student**, and then you're the teacher."

"Be a **student** of the system, and teach others to be **students** of the system and your success are assured."

All of this talk about being a student made me a little nervous. You see, if you were to describe Johnna Briatta (yes, that is my maiden name, not an Italian pasta dish), the word "student" would not have been in the description.

I attended a private Catholic High School for girls. Yes, all girls! Actually, it was great that I didn't have to worry about what to wear each day because of the uniforms, and there were no "boy" distractions. It was an environment that would allow me to give my full attention to my studies. Right? Not! My teachers would often use the phrase, "she doesn't apply herself". Very true when it came to studying, but very untrue when it came to having a very exciting social life. When my friends were planning and preparing for the test that week, I was planning and preparing for the party that weekend. I was having a ball and…I was good at it!

### *There are no shortcuts to the top*

The school had a pom-pom squad, yet no cheerleading squad. My sophomore year, they decided to add a cheerleading squad. We had a brother school and we would cheer for all of their football and basketball games. I did do some cheerleading when I was in grammar school, so this was a fit for me. I tried out, and made the Varsity Squad.

Because the squad was so brand new, the school decided to send us to a special cheerleading camp that summer, one that would prepare us the for the next school year. It would be an entire week to learn the ins and outs of the cheerleading world, hosted at a college a couple hundred miles away.

All the parents signed the permission slips, and off we went, by bus, to the college. By the way, did I mention that we did not have a chaperone from our school, just the Varsity Squad captain, a senior by the name Maria Romanucci (not her real name, but you get the point)?

Needless to say, we were not prepared for the world of cheerleading. Every morning, all squads had to meet on the lawn. All of the participating squads had colorful uniforms, with matching hair ribbons. We wore our gym uniforms. (I wish I was kidding.) We were labeled the "bad news cheerleaders" because some of the members of our squad smoked cigarettes during the morning exercises. The entire week of gymnastics and routines were in preparation for the big competition at the end of the week. I am not proud to say that we came in last place, dead last.

On the way home, the bus ride was on the quiet side, until Maria perked up and said, "They say we came in last place, I say we came in first!" Of course, we were confused as to what she was saying. Then she added "How would they ever know we came in last, we were the only ones there? I say we are champions!" With that, the diabolical plan was construed. We became First Place winners in the cheerleading competition. Maria, who had access to her parents' credit card, went to a trophy store and purchased the largest trophy. It stood several feet tall, had pillars and a large gold cup at the top.

The lie started to take on a life of its own. It got bigger and bigger and bigger. Our parents thought we were winners. Our school was so proud that they scheduled a pep rally in honor of our accomplishment. A local newspaper did a story on us. They even had to cut the glass in the trophy cabinet at school to make room for the monster trophy.

The "win" was empty. It was a fabricated lie that got out of control. I increasingly became uncomfortable with all of the praise because we didn't deserve it. I started to lose sleep at night. I felt guilty for being deceptive. Guilt, the gift that keeps on giving.

Within weeks, we were found out and made an example of for our entire school and local community to see. At first, the scheme seemed funny, actually quite brilliant. As it unraveled, I realized how many people we mislead, and how we hurt them by not being truthful with them. I was humiliated, especially because these were the people that would have been supportive of us, even if we were in last place. There are no shortcuts to the top.

## Reality sets in

I met my student guidance counselor for the first time during my Senior Year. Not a good start. I sat across her desk as she began in a somber and serious tone, "Johnna, you are taking six classes." I had to interrupt and question, "I am?" She continued, "You are failing all six". This was a blow to me, especially because my parents were already planning a great graduation party. This would have definitely put a damper on the party.

I suddenly realized the severity of the situation and talked with all of my teachers. Did I say, "Talk?" OK…beg. I did graduate, by the skin of my teeth. I was even accepted to a couple of colleges, I do realize that sometimes colleges simply need the money.

I attended several different colleges in a matter of a few years, and had selected around 12 different majors. My parents kept their belief in me, hoping that I would find my way. The last straw came when, after attending a concert the night before, I went downstairs in the morning to find my parents at the kitchen table. I announced with all of the conviction that I previously announced all of my chosen career paths, and proudly stated, "Mom, Dad, I have finally figured it out!" My mother looked to me and said, "Again?" "Yes, I want to be … a drummer!"

With that revelation, my college days were numbered and I attempted a variety of career paths. I couldn't figure out what and who I wanted to be when I grew up. Or you could say that I was becoming a really good quitter. When something would get uncomfortable or become too difficult, I would simply throw in the towel and go try something else – never really testing my ability, or giving myself a chance to succeed.

## Entering the workforce

A friend suggested that I go to a placement firm to help me discover a career path, or simply just get a job. I found a firm that specialized in hiring sales people earning six figures or above. Now, I wasn't a sales person, technically, although I did sell my parents on 12 majors and three colleges. And I certainly wasn't earning six figures or more, but that was a good number to start, I thought.

I contacted the placement firm and experienced a brief phone interview. When asked if I was earning six figures and above, I simply stated, "I am on track to do that." Now, she didn't know that I was just stepping on the track, and I didn't feel it necessary to share that. I was granted an interview.

My resumé was short and sweet and said a lot about what I was capable of, even though I had yet to display any of these redeeming qualities. In the interview, the counselor looked at me, looked down at the resumé, then looked back at me, then down at the resumé, then back again. She then said, "You are grossly under qualified for all of our clients." With that kind of statement, what could I possibly say, other than, "Thank you?"

After some more discussion, she wound up liking my personality and let me know that a sales assistant position just opened up. I took the job on the spot, even though the pay wasn't very good; the job had potential to be a stepping-stone to being a corporate recruiter, and that position had the potential to pay the six figures that I was "on track" for in the first place.

I never had a dream of being in that industry, I just happened to land in that industry on a fluke interview. It's not that I didn't like it, but I didn't necessarily love it either. It was simply, a job. I stayed there for several years, and did work my way up to recruiter, rookie of the year, and later management. During that time I had married and had become pregnant with my first daughter, Sabrina.

I was in a financial situation that allowed me to have a choice of staying home once I had my baby. My mother was a stay at home mom and I wanted to be one also. I wanted to do the right thing with the company I was with, so I thought it would be best to let them know ahead of time so that I could teach my replacement. I made them aware that I was not coming back after my pregnancy leave.

After this was known through the upper level management, I was summoned to meet with one of the vice-presidents. She asked me, "So, is it true? Are you really not coming back so that you can stay home and play mommy?" I was stunned at the disgust in her voice. She then added, "What a tremendous waste of talent." I know what you are thinking: how could this woman possibly say something like that? I figured that she was having a bad day. Maybe she was still upset about the house falling on her sister.

I was a stay at home mom for five years. When I was faced with becoming a single mom, I automatically thought that I would have to go back to corporate recruiting. I didn't know anything else. I never achieved a college degree, which also made my options very limited as far as earning potential. What I did know was that going back to that profession meant long hours and daycare for my girls who were 2 and 4 years old at the time.

## The day that changed my life

It is amazing how our lives are made up of thin strings – these little connections and events that happen each day that often lead us to something or someone. This was one of those days. This was the day when I was at my kitchen table reviewing a job offer from my prior company: a seven-page manuscript of what was expected of me and my job responsibilities. The seven pages were quite overwhelming, but not as overwhelming as the list that lay right next to the job offer. It was a list of reputable daycare providers. I was preparing to call each one and set up appointments to see who would be the most qualified to care for Sabrina and Monica 8-10 hours a day.

It was on this day that my phone rang, and someone called me out of the blue, fired up about his new business. I had known Matt from previous business experiences; we had been involved in a couple of "practice" network marketing companies. One of them, he hit the very highest of achievement levels. However, he left the industry completely when he had become disheartened with the business practices of the company that he was representing. He was currently working in corporate America and quickly realized that it wasn't the answer. He was willing to take a chance on another company because he believed in the industry, and he knew that it worked.

I wasn't against the industry; in fact, I loved the basic concept that a good solid network marketing business is based on: "If you help enough people get what they want, you will always get what you want." My only disappointment was that I had never really found the right company to represent, or at least one that would pay substantially immediately. Nevertheless, he was convinced and sold out, and his enthusiasm is what provoked my curiosity. He three-way called a recorded message, I listened to that, he then introduced me to a couple of his business partners and they simply shared what their experience had been. One of the gentleman simply said, "My wife and I can work from home." That was all I needed to hear. I wanted to take a look.

Matt was so convinced that this was the real deal, and that he was going to make a fortune with this company, I decided to go with him to one of the events that was happening. This teaching event was a great way for me to see the whole picture of the company, and also get a better understanding on how the business worked.

The event was an 11-hour car ride from where we lived. Now, the fact of the matter is, an 11-hour car ride is a long way from home. It was very inconvenient. That is a fact.

### *When the reason and the dream are big enough, the facts don't count.*

If I wanted to change my life, I had to make the changes, and do what was necessary to learn how to make the changes.

Matt was working in his job full time and the event was on Saturday. The plan was for Matt to pick me up after work; we would drive through the night, and be there on Saturday morning. Now I understand, this was a little *inconvenient*, and the fact is we were probably going to be a little tired on Saturday.

### *When the reason and the dream are big enough, the facts don't count.*

We drove through the night, and arrived at the event in just enough time to quickly change in the bathroom, and grab some breakfast. We sat in the front row. Matt took notes, I sat and watched. They showed how the business worked, but what really got me fired up were the people who were experiencing success with the business. They all had different backgrounds, were from different walks of life, from homeowners to business owners, blue collar to white collar. All of them had one thing in common: they were achieving their goals and dreams through this business. The business was allowing them to have choices in their life.

I wanted a choice. I wanted to be able to be a stay at home mom *and* make a big income. If this can happen for them; why not me? *If one person can; any person can.* The most important things that I felt after the meeting was *hope,* simply hope, and an *amazing feeling of opportunity.*

It reminded me of a story I once read about a tourist who paused to rest in a small town in the mountains. He went over to an old man sitting on a bench in front of the only store in town and asked him, "Sir, what is this town known for?" The old man looked up and said, "I don't rightly know, except that it's the starting point to the world. You can start here, and go anywhere you want."

## The three ingredients

At my first business overview, I was told that in order to be successful, I had to have three ingredients. These ingredients were not only important for me to be successful; it was important for the members of my organization to have the three ingredients as well. It is like a lock and key combination. All three ingredients are necessary for your success and the success of your team.

**1. Burning desire**. Burning desire is not a wish, this is not a hope, and it is not a "maybe I will *try*". Burning desire can't be given to anyone, and it cannot be taught. Desire comes from within. This is the desire to change something in your life. Burning desire is a deep-down burn in your belly. It is the type of burn that keeps you up at night because you are thrilled about going after your dream. This is the emotional juice that keeps you going when the going gets tough.

What is your desire? What do you want? What is your dream? What are you aspiring to? What kind of life do you want to live? The people that were having success at the meeting that I attended had a clear-cut vision of what they wanted for their life, what they wanted for their family: they were focused on that reality, and kept going until they achieved that reality.

*People are happiest when they are in the process of achieving something of importance. Taking action, creating momentum, and knowing we are on the right track creates an incredible enthusiasm and zest for life.*

**2. Willingness to work**. It's called work for a reason. Are you willing to roll up your sleeves and go to work? Work is not a four-letter word. Work is not a bad thing, or a negative thing. Work takes on a whole other meaning when you are working toward something of importance to you, not just a paycheck. You have to be willing to work smarter, not harder, and be consistent.

*As Jim Rohn says, "Work full time on your job, or in your traditional business, work part time on your fortune."*

**3. Teachable**. You have to be willing to follow a proven system, a formula of success laid out by those that have the lifestyle and income that you would like. This is very important.

The most important question is *who* are you going to take counsel from? Make sure that you are taking counsel from those that have built a successful business with the company that you are with, and those that are in your up-line structure. This industry is filled with network marketing gurus that have NEVER built a successful network marketing business or haven't been in the trenches in many years; yet, they are filled with advice of how you should do it.

*Be a student of the system, and then teach others to be students of the system, and your success is assured.*

There it was again, that word that made me cringe: "student". When we attended the events, Matt would be taking notes like crazy; I would go to the events and smile at the speakers, not taking a single note, and actually think that I got it. I actually believed that I would remember it all.

One time, on our way home from a meeting, we stopped to get something to eat. I was excited, as usual. I tried to remember some of the great things that I had learned that day. I wanted to share them with Matt. I said, "What was that thing that was said about commitment? Boy, that was really good." Matt pulled his notebook out of his briefcase, flipped through the pages and read, "Commitment is doing the thing you said you would do long after the mood you said it in has passed." I said, "Yes, that's it; that was really good! I also like the thing about the mountain, umm I am on the mountain, and someone is dying on the mountain. How did that go?" Matt flipped through his notes and found the quote that I had butchered: "You will find me at the top of the mountain, or dead on the side, but I am not going back to where I was." "Yes" I said, "that's the one!"

Matt then shut his notebook and looked at me very seriously and said, "Johnna, how do you expect things to change in your life, if you don't make any changes? How can you teach others, if you are not even being taught yourself? You didn't take a single note and you expect to understand? How can you build a huge business if you are not treating it like one? You cannot give to your team what you do not have." So, I said, "I am not familiar with *taking* notes, I am familiar with *passing* notes!" He then said, "For things to change, I had to change, you will have to also. You are not doing this business for a grade, you are doing it for your daughters; you are doing it for your life."

*I then said,*
*"You take notes as if your life depends on it."*
*He answered,*
*"It does!"*

From that moment on, I took notes and became a *student*. I listened and took in all of the knowledge of the leaders of the business that had the income and lifestyle that I was striving for. I didn't just take notes and stick them in a drawer; I took the notes, reviewed them, and implemented what I had learned.

I also started to read books. I was not a reader at that time in my life. I wasn't book smart. I was more magazine smart. I kept hearing in my head,

*"For things to change, I have to change.*
*For things to get better, I have to become better."*

I read books that would add value to my life so that I in turn could add value to others.

I became a reader. I started out with just 15 minutes a day in a positive book. It then grew from there: I have since developed a passion for acquiring knowledge and understanding, and am often reading several books at a time. I have read hundreds of books over the years.

*The more I read, the more I grow personally,*
*the better leader I become, the bigger my business grows.*
*It all goes together.*

The philosophies and teachings become a part of who you are. They affect the way you think and the way you act. They affect the way you react to things, whether they are good or bad. Most importantly, good books will affect your attitude. In a negative world, I needed to put positive things in my head every day to keep me on track. You cannot give what you do not have; you cannot export what you have not imported. The more I learned, the more I wanted to learn.

*One thing that I do know for sure,*
*Formal education will make you a living;*
*Self education will make you a fortune.*
*Today, I am a millionaire.*
*I am a self-educated woman, and I am proud of it.*

## Are you teachable?

Everyone who enters the world of network marketing will always go through three phases of learning. Some will only make it to two, and stall out their business because of their own personal lack of growth.

## Phase 1 – "I know nothing"

This is a wonderful phase. This is when someone is a sponge and excited to learn. They are open for direction and coaching. This is when someone is listening to educational audios, conference calls, following the system and process of the business, reading books, taking notes at events and putting those notes into action.

They are consistently following the success formula. They incorporate the up-line leadership in the process and are allowing the coach to lead them in the right and most profitable direction. The words, "yeah, but.." are not part of their vocabulary. They realize if they just copy what the leaders have done and take action, they will get the same results. The results are duplication, and strong duplication results in success and big income.

## Phase 2 – "I know everything"

This is a very dangerous phase. The crazy thing is, EVERYONE hits this phase. The question is, "Will you survive it?" It is ironic that the success of someone in Phase 1 will often lead to Phase 2. Not being teachable is often rooted in achievement. Some people mistakenly believe that if they accomplish a goal, or have some success, they no longer have to learn or grow. They essentially become "know it alls". This is when the notebook gets put away, when mingling happens in the back of the room when a meeting is taking place or, worse yet, hallway seminars are conducted.

If you ask someone in Phase 2, "What book are you reading?" they will not have an answer. The person stops doing all of the activity that brought them success in the first place; then they wonder why their results are not the same.

*John Maxwell writes, "Your growth determines who you are, who you are determines who you will attract, who you attract determines the success of your team."*

The greatest leaders are perpetual learners. If you want to attract, keep and grow leaders, *you* have to remain a student, *you* have to remain teachable.

It is easy to distinguish those that are in Phase 2. They will begin to isolate themselves from the whole. Instead of THE team, it becomes MY team. It is around this time when their business stops growing on all levels. This is a very critical time because there are only two options. The first option is to play the blame game. They will begin to blame their up-line, their team, their company, whatever is easy to point a finger at. For many, it is easier to blame, than take responsibility for failure. They become negative and feel that they are justified in voicing their negativity to anyone who will listen.

Earlier I said that EVERYONE hits Phase 2, including us. For a short time, we thought we were better, stronger and more brilliant than our up-line. Fortunately for us and the growth of our business, we didn't stay in this egocentric state for long.

Everyone in your up-line leadership has a role to play in your success. *You* can choose *which* role they play. Everyone brings a unique and different asset to the table. You can discover those assets in the leaders of your up-line, and use those assets for the betterment of your business, which benefits the whole team.

We admire and respect those that have built the business before us for, if it wasn't for them, we would not be here, living an amazing and wonderful life. And for that, I am eternally grateful.

Those that stay in Phase 2 will either choose to stay on the negative path, have stagnant business growth and possibly quit out of frustration, or look deep within them and come to the astonishing realization of Phase 3.

## Phase 3 – "I don't know everything"

Being teachable requires us to admit that we don't know everything. We have to remain humble enough to take coaching and counsel from those that have the success that we are striving for. This requires us to be open to new ideas, especially if they are not our own.

When you exit Phase 2, and the sooner the better, everything changes overnight. Your relationships with leaders that are also in Phase 3 will become stronger and quite valuable. You can constantly bounce ideas off each other and learn from each other. There are seldom ego struggles in this phase: no one is trying to protect their title, seniority or position. You become equals, peers, true partners, with the common goal of making things better for the good of all.

*You can agree to disagree because conflict, when coupled with love and respect, will always equal growth.*

When the student is ready, the teacher will appear. The greatest leaders are perpetual learners and perpetual doers. The more we learn, and the more books we read, the more we realize how much we don't know. The more that you grow and learn as the leader, the more your team will grow and learn.

*Don't strive to be a king and run a dynasty.*
*Strive to be a king maker and override many dynasties.*

# Chapter 4

# Where there is a Will, there is a Way

### Temporary inconveniences

**When I started to build my network marketing business, I knew that I was going to have to make some changes in my life in order to fit this in.** My daughters were 2 and 4 years old at that time. Their normal bedtime was 9:00 p.m. Their bedtime routine was bath and then I would read them stories before bed. How was I going to be able to do this, and make the phone calls that needed to be made in order for me to build the business?

The next morning I woke up and decided that the girls would skip their naps that day. We did the normal bedtime routine, except they were in bed by 6:30 p.m.! Now, the fact of the matter is when you put children to bed at 6:30 p.m., they wake up REAL early.

*But when the dream is big enough, the facts don't count.*

I had to be willing to make TEMPORARY changes. I had to be able to put up with TEMPORARY inconveniences for a LIFETIME of convenience.

### *Where there is a will, there is a way.*

As I started to build the business, I started earning income immediately; in fact, I earned income my first week. This was exciting, except I was still in a financial hole. I was in major credit card debt because, as a single mom, I was living on credit cards. It is amazing how much you can put on credit cards, gas for my car, clothing for my daughters and food from the grocery store. I am not proud of that, but that was my reality at that time in my life.

### Big belief will build big business

A major convention was coming up and Matt had encouraged me to go. He understood the value of what a convention could do, not only for information and education, but also for my belief. If my belief was big, I would build a big business. I had told Matt that things were pretty tight, and I wasn't sure if I would be able to do it. He didn't allow me to negotiate my success away, he simply said,

### *"I believe you are a winner, and winners always find a way."*

I filled out the form for the weekend convention and put my credit card down.

A few days later, my phone rang. It was the convention company calling; apparently my credit card did not go through. I told them to hold on for a moment, I ran to get my purse, and retrieved the stack of credit cards. I got back on the phone and instructed them how to break down the amount over three different credit cards.

Now, I know for most people reading this you are thinking, "obviously you couldn't afford it, it obviously cost too much."

***You see, it didn't cost too much. Nothing costs too much! I didn't have enough money!***

I couldn't afford not going. How was my financial situation going to change if I didn't make an attempt to learn how to change it? What is the cost of the event *not* attended? What is the cost of the book *not* read?

Was the event worth attending? Of course: I have yet to miss a major national convention of the company I represent. Was the event informative? Yes. Was the event educational? Yes. Was the event inspirational? Yes. But it wasn't the event itself that had the major impact on my life. It was then that I realized that I was willing to do whatever it took to make the business work for me.

***Where there is a will, there is a way.***

Matt wasn't my husband then, he was my business partner, mentor and my friend, who believed in me. I liked him so much that I set him up with some of my

51

friends. I thought he was such a wonderful man. Upon attempting to help him enhance his love life, he would sternly look at me and say, "Make sure you let her know that I am NEVER getting married again and I don't do kids." This was one of his favorite sayings. He said it so often that I believed him, never even thinking that our friendship would turn into something else

Well, have you heard the saying "Never say never"? After working together for about a year, Matt professed his love for me. I was in shock with what was coming out of the dedicated bachelor's mouth. I couldn't deny my feelings for him and, within a month, we were married. Instead of our courtship being dinner dates and movie nights, our "courtship" was business presentations, meetings and events. On our wedding day, our preacher, who was also in business with us, proclaimed, "Now, you two… go get two, go forth and multiply!"

## Some inventory required

At a company convention, Matt and I had purchased several business tools that were necessary for the growth of our business. We spent several hundred dollars, which was a stretch at the time, but we knew how important it was to *treat our business like a business*. We invited our team up into our suite that evening and instead of putting the boxes of tools in the closet, Matt chose to leave them in the entrance hallway of our room. He wanted the people that entered our room to have to step over them in order to enter. I certainly wasn't thrilled with this idea, and didn't understand what he was doing.

When people arrived, they walked around these boxes that were rudely in their way. One person asked about them. Matt knew this would happen. He pointed to the boxes and said, "That is my future! I am taking this business all the way. What are you doing?" One then said, "I haven't made much money yet, I can't spend more than I have made yet." Matt responded, "A farmer never questions the need for seed; a farmer can only pray for rain. Business tools are the rain maker, they are the change maker. Treat your part-time business like a business, not a hobby, and it will pay you like a business. Treat it like a BIG business, and it will pay you like a BIG business."

Some went and bought more business tools; others chose to ignore the advice and then wondered why their business didn't grow. The hobbyists will always chose to quit their network marketing business claiming that their business didn't pay them enough. The fact is the business paid them exactly how they treated it, like a hobby.

## Owning it all

Debt has created more problems and challenges for families than any other issue. It causes marriage problems, emotional problems, spiritual problems, physical problems. We wanted to eliminate all of our debt. Our goal was to become good stewards of our money.

***Being in debt is a habit, being broke is a result of that habit. People are broke because they think broke.***

We eliminated this habit and way of thinking, and changed our financial life completely.

After Matt and I had married, we purchased a lovely 3-bedroom town house in a suburb of Chicago. Sabrina and Monica shared a room, and the third bedroom was our office. The room was so small that we removed the closet doors so that we could squeeze in two desks. Even though our network marketing business was paying us well, we were still climbing out of the debt. I am amazed at how many people I have seen in this industry, start making a tremendous amount of money and, instead of getting rid of their current debt, they bring their debt up, essentially becoming broke at a higher level!

Matt developed a formula and we stuck with this formula. It requires discipline and a deep understanding that all "material" things do not need to be acquired immediately. They can wait, and when the time comes and you can purchase those items in their entirety, the reward is that much sweeter. The formula is as follows: 25% of our income went to taxes, 25% went to our debt, (this eventually becomes savings and investments,) 25% went back into our network marketing business, business supplies & travel expenses, 15% went for rewards, and 10% we tithed to our favorite charity, mission or church.

Remember when I said it takes discipline? A few months into our marriage, I was in need of a new car. My current automobile was in poor shape and we were starting to have some engine trouble. Matt decided to take the matter into his hands; he left in the morning in my car, and came home with a white Chevy Lumina with red interior. It had several thousand miles on it. This was NOT my dream car! It was most definitely not the car that I had envisioned myself behind the wheel of. Before I could express my dismay, Matt put a slip of paper in my hands. It was a document that I was completely unfamiliar with because I had never seen one before. It was the title. He held it up and said, "Johnna, we own this car, not the bank, it's ours!"

We have adopted this philosophy for everything that we purchase. If we can't pay for it in full, we simply don't buy it until we can. When we do use plastic, the amounts are paid for at the end of each month.

Today, we have a beautifully furnished home, luxury cars, motorcycles, fine pieces of art, designer clothing, exceptional jewelry, and have taken world class vacations around the world. Most importantly, we have been able to give abundantly to our favorite charities and missions.

You too can become a good steward of your money. It simply will take a mental shift, some focus and discipline.

Anything is possible if the will is strong enough. Any challenge can be overcome. Any obstacle can be conquered. Any dilemma can be solved. You simply have to WANT TO.

We have amazing and unconquerable spirits. We were designed for greatness. We were put on this earth to live an amazing life.

Where there is a will, there will ALWAYS be a way!

# Chapter 5

# Proper Protocol

**Imagine your business as the "Goose that Lays the Golden Egg". Imagine your business being a living and breathing goose.** If you did have a goose that laid golden eggs, you would do anything and everything to protect the goose. You would feed the goose, take care of the goose and protect the goose from any harm. Your goose is living and breathing. Your network marketing business is living and breathing also, because it consists of people. Anything that is living and breathing can be fragile.

There are rules of the industry, codes of conduct and codes of ethics, that are meant to protect your business: they are meant to protect your goose and keep your goose healthy and growing.

What is the one thing that every member of your team needs to build their business and get them to their dreams and goals?

## Belief

Belief is defined as: A state or habit of mind in which trust or confidence is placed in some person or thing; to have a firm conviction as to the reality or goodness of something; to accept as truth.

Your team's belief is the single most important element in them achieving success. There is one Golden Rule that I feel is the most important. This is the rule that is so often overlooked. This is the rule that many don't even realize they are breaking. Leaders will single-handedly chip away at their own team's belief. We have seen organizations plummet and go away. We have seen many dreams of innocent team mates being shattered by ignorance.

## Rule #1 Negatives ALWAYS go UP

I will give you some examples. Let's say, for instance, you have a new business partner, and they are starting to work their business. They call you up because they have had a frustrating day, and you say, "yeah, me too!" They are drowning, looking for you to throw them a life preserver, and you jump in the raging waters with them! This is not the scenario where misery loves company. If you need a pep talk, take your challenge to your up-line. *Never* lean on your team for motivation.

*Anyone can be up when they are up;*
*a leader is up when they are down.*

You have to be the cheerleader for the members of your team. You have to be the person who brings them back to their reason for building the business. You have to be the person who lets them know that you believe in them and that tomorrow is another day. They must get off of the phone with *you* charged up, fired up and ready to begin again.

Another example is when someone goes to a meeting, and feels that it's important everyone in the meeting knows that their guest didn't show up. Matt and I have had many guests not show; however, we were the only ones who knew it. We took responsibility, we know what went wrong. *We* did not get our prospect's belief big enough for them to make the meeting a priority. When a member of your team has a prospect that doesn't show up, don't simply say, "Well, that is part of the game, mine didn't show up either" or tear them down for not following the proper invite process. Simply ask this question: "Why do you think that is?" Let them think about it for themselves and self-correct.

A critical comment about the company that you represent, fellow leaders or the product line to *anyone* who is on your team will chip away at their belief, which in essence will stop them in their tracks. When belief is gone, the list gets put away; the phone is not picked up and the income-producing activity stops.

I am shocked at how many of those in network marketing shoot at their own goose. They feel that it is imperative to protect their teammates from a negative prospect when *they* are the ones who are the culprit spewing negativity.

Not spreading negative comments to your team doesn't just protect your income; most importantly, it protects theirs.

The challenge for some is that they have brought family and close friends into the business with them. That is great! Share everything with them, except negatives. Never forget that you are now in business with them, and by expressing criticism, gossip and slander you are essentially hurting *them* in pursuit of *their* dream.

Matt and I no longer verbalize negatives. We do not participate in gossip or slander. We have trained ourselves, through studying leadership to become solution thinkers. Anyone can gripe, complain and whine: a leader focuses on solutions.

### How do you kill an entire flock of geese?

De-edification is a killer and will not just kill *your* goose; it can kill an *entire flock* of geese.

> *To de-edify is to tear someone down.*
> *To edify is to lift someone up.*

De-edification will take on many forms. It can be a raised eyebrow, a snide comment, a put down or an outright negative comment about someone. This type of behavior can destroy a significant portion of *your* credibility.

De-edification of anyone in your up-line to any member of your team will do irreparable damage to your organization. You have given your team free rein to do the same to you, and then their team will do the same to them. This behavior leads to an environment that is filled with pettiness and back-stabbing, instead of a positive environment that will fuel growth.

Unfortunately, there are people that feel it is necessary to tear down someone else's house to build their own. The only time they can feel good about themselves is to talk badly about others. This behavior gives them a false sense of superiority. Jealousy and envy are very powerful and negative emotions that cause people to do less than honorable things. These people are in desperate need of personal growth.

No matter what the reason, it is very important to understand that everyone on your team wants long-term income and security. *Security comes from stability.* When children see their parents fighting, they naturally assume things aren't good and feelings of insecurity arise. A known struggle between two leaders can tear a team apart.

I do understand that we are in a people business. The joy of the business is working with people; the absolute frustration of this business is working with those very same people. We didn't always agree with our up-line and sometimes we agreed to disagree; but we grew to respect them and realized that we wouldn't be here without them.

You may not agree with someone in your up-line or a fellow leader; it really doesn't matter, the rest of your team shouldn't hear about it, unless you truly want to hurt them in order to fuel your own ego. Take your challenge to your up-line leadership and fix it. You can find a redeeming quality in *everyone*.

We can go back to the philosophy my mother taught me, "If you don't have anything nice to say, don't say anything at all." When someone approaches me with negative dirt about someone, the first thing I think is, "I wonder what they are saying about me when my back is turned."

Always keep in mind that what you do will always duplicate, good or bad. If you are trashing others, you have given your team free rein to do it to you, and it gives their team free rein to do it to them, this will spread through your goose like a cancer.

### Shooting your neighbor's goose

Shooting your neighbor's goose is taking negativity to a person who is cross-line. Cross-line means that their volume is not in your business, and your production volume is not in their business. Taking negatives cross-line is not only hurting that person's belief, it is shooting someone else's goose. I equate this to coveting thy neighbor's goods. Do unto others as you would have them do unto you. You wouldn't want someone dumping on people in your team: don't do it to theirs.

Counseling or coaching someone who is not in your team can also do damage to someone else's organization. If you are not in the up-line structure, you should always lead the person to someone who is in the up-line. They have a vested interest in that person's long-term success and income.

## Edification is the key!

When edification is practiced, the environment is fertile for growth, fun and leadership development. Edification is to lift each other up and treat each other with respect. We are all God's children. We are imperfect. We have all made mistakes and all have faults; by the same token we all have incredible redeeming qualities.

When edification is practiced by you, it will also duplicate throughout your organization. You edify others, your team edifies others, and their team edifies others, and so on. People want to be part of a team that is having fun, a team that respects each other to the theme of "All for one and one for all".

## Never forget where you came from

I remember my first network marketing convention. I was with a "practice" company, and it was at that event that I fell in love with this industry. An industry of people helping people, what a concept! This industry was where I wanted to be. The company, as it turned out, was not the right one for me, although, the convention was impressive. I was suprised at the thousands of people that were in attendance, and the positive attitude of those in the crowd.

All of the speakers that took the stage were informative and educational; however, the two that had the most impact on me were two of the female leaders of the company. I could relate to them. They inspired me!

After the day session was over, I exited the convention center and started heading toward my room. I happened to see one of the speakers; she was just a few steps ahead of me. I got up the courage to meet her, shake her hand and share with her the impact that she had on me. As I approached her, I extended my hand and said, "I just wanted to meet you and share with you how much of an impact you had on me today. Thank you." She abruptly shook my hand, looked around the room, never looked at me and said very quickly, "I am glad you liked it." She walked off, leaving me in the dust, feeling inadequate. I thought to myself, wow, I could never achieve her level of "stardom"!

I continued to walk down the massive hallways outside of the convention center, feeling like a dejected nobody. As I continued to walk, I glanced across the hallway and saw the second speaker. She had a crowd gathered around her. She was smiling, laughing and shaking hands. I was compelled to go and meet her. As I approached I saw how this woman was engaging everyone, and looking in their eyes. I stood behind a couple of rows of people waiting to shake her hand. She then greeted me with a genuine, sincere smile, "Hi, I'm Sue, what is your name?" I thought to myself, "I know who YOU are!" I was struck by the warmth and lack of arrogance. She greeted me as a person, as an equal. "My name is Johnna; I just wanted to let you know that your talk really inspired me. Thank you." She then said, "Thank you, Johnna, that means so much to me, it was so nice of you to let me know. So where are you from?" What? Did she actually ask a question about *me*? We then talked for a few moments. She asked me who my up-line leadership was and, even though I was not in her organization, she edified my up-line, making me feel proud of the team that I was on.

I walked away feeling important and special. This short meeting had a dynamic impact on how I meet and greet people at meetings and conventions. I bring myself back to that first convention that I attended, and the profound difference in how each of the women made me feel. I often wonder what would have happened to my network marketing journey if I had never met the second female leader. I later found out that even though these two leaders shared the same title of achieving the top level of the company, their difference in income was several millions of dollars.

**When you achieve great things in this industry, you will be recognized for your achievements.**

**People will start to think that you are a star. That is not the problem.**

**The problem is when YOU start to think that you are a star.**

NEVER forget how you began. NEVER forget how unsure of yourself you were in the beginning. NEVER forget where you came from. A simple handshake and a smile can mean a world of difference to someone, as it did for me.

If proper protocol is practiced, your team will run like a *well-oiled, happy and productive machine.* Can you *make* people do the right thing? The answer to that question is "no".

*The only actions that we can control are our own. Let it begin with you. You be the change that you want to see in your organization, and that will catch on, grow and spread throughout your team.*

# Chapter 6

# What are You Thinking?

**We have always encouraged people to start a dream board or a vision board.** This is a board with visual aids of the things that you want in your life – a simple visualization of what you want your life to look like. This gives you targets to shoot for. Everything that Matt and I have achieved over the last decade started out on this board. There is something very powerful about visualization and *seeing* the life that you are striving for.

Several years ago, a woman, who was on our team, came over for a visit. I brought her into our home office, and showed her our dream board. I was excited to share with her the dreams that Matt and I had. I then asked her, "What is on your board?" She replied, "I don't have a dream board." I asked her, "Why not?" She then said, "I don't want anything." I asked, "You don't want *anything, nothing?*" She looked down and a tear started to roll down her cheek. She replied, "I don't *want* to *want* anything, because I don't believe I can ever have them. I don't want to set myself up for disappointment."

This is the main reason why so many achieve so little. She *believed* that she could never have anything more, so therefore she was living out those beliefs.Now, goal setting and desire are two very different things. Some believe that if you simply write things down, that's goal setting. It is not. Goals have to become what you *believe* and, most importantly, what you *expect*. You will get what you expect, every time, without fail. Henry Ford wrote, "If you think you can or you think you can't, you are right." Goals have to become beliefs and expectations.

### *You have to believe what you want is absolutely inevitable.*

In order to become a millionaire you must first begin to *think* like a millionaire. We had to treat our business like a multi-million dollar business so it would pay us like a multi-million dollar business. We had to get our heads right. We *studied* success and leadership by reading books about success and leadership. We started reading magazines like *The Robb Report*, *Condé Nast Traveller* and *Architectural Digest*. Why? Because these are the magazines that millionaires read about luxury lifestyles.

Cut pictures out of things that you want, and places that you want to go, people you want to help, and charities or missions that you want to support. I look at our board daily because it is hanging up in our home office. When things are achieved, we gladly take them down. But, most importantly, we replace with something else.

**A goal achieved ceases to motivate.
If you stop striving, you stop living.**

The biggest mistake I see people make is once they achieve a dream, they stop striving. It is important to always have a big dream. Whenever you achieve something, replace that dream with a new one. The mere fact that you attained one dream is proof that it can be done again and again and again. Don't rest on your laurels.

By staying focused on your dream and your reasons, it gives every phone call you make a purpose, it gives every presentation you make a purpose. You will now have purpose driven business activity with a knowing that every little thing you do is taking you one step closer.

The concept of visualizing a dream and achieving that dream has happened in our life over and over again. One profound example is when Matt and I were first married. We were living in a 3-bedroom townhouse and we had a picture of the house that we wanted to live in on our refrigerator. Every morning, when I woke up, and went downstairs into the kitchen, I would look at that picture. I would imagine living in the house. I imagined having Sunday dinners with our family, I imagined having wonderful parties, I imagined having Christmas gatherings, I imagined having a home office, I imagined a large gourmet kitchen, I imagined a great room, I imagined having a library full of books, I imagined a fitness center and spa, a home theater, and guest rooms for our out-of-town friends. I visualized living in such a house.

One day, Matt had said, let's go look at some land and find the property to build the house we wanted. We were so specific in what we wanted that we believed we could not just *find it*; we would have to *build it*. As we stood on a vacant plot of land, a man pulled up to us in his truck and said, "I have driven by you a couple of times today, I sat in my driveway, and something made me come talk to you. I normally don't do this, but I am a custom builder. I built a large home for my family several years ago, my wife and I have since downsized. This home has been on the market for a while and the real estate contract has just ended. Would you like to look at it?" Matt asked him, "Where is it?" We were surprised to find out that it was in the exact town where Matt grew up, and much of his family lived there.

The next day we decided to meet this man at the house. When we pulled up to the driveway, I got so excited: it was beautiful! As I exclaimed my joy, Matt sternly looked at me and said, "Johnna, we are dealing with the owner, if you do that again, you are staying the car!!"

As we walked through the house, I looked past the decorating, the tile and wallpaper, and focused on the house itself. The house had a home office, a great room, a library, extra rooms for guests, a large kitchen, and room for a fitness center, spa and home theater. I walked outside to see beautiful tree-lined property. I was fired up, but I wasn't saying a thing. I was working on my poker face when I walked back into the house to find Matt and the owner: Matt was loudly expressing, "This is EVERYTHING we wanted!"

Now came the moment of truth: the price. The home was originally priced at nearly $1 million. At the time, this was a little more than we were willing to do. We were newly out of debt and did not want to become broke at a higher level. We simply did not want to live for a house. The man then said, "I believe there was a reason why I was led to talk to you. You are nice kids. I want you to have my house. What can you afford?"

*It was at this moment that I understood the power of the dream board and visualization.* It works, and it will work again and again and again. Because we had the vision and goal in front of us for approximately four years, our daily actions reflected that goal. Our income was increasing over those years and our business started to flourish and we were making more money than we had ever in our entire life. It would have been easy for us to spend, spend and spend; instead we saved, saved and saved. Opportunity met preparedness, and we were able not only to buy the home, but renovate it to our own specifications.

It is funny that the naysayers will always be the naysayers. When we first moved into our home, we had someone over for a visit. As they were getting their tour, they asked, "Why do you need a house this big?" Matt said, "I don't". They then asked, "Then why in the world would you buy a house this big?" and Matt simply said, "Because I can."

## Not in the dreaming mood?

When I first started to attend events, I would hear the speakers say, "You have to dream big! Get your dream back. A dream is a wish your heart makes. If you have a big dream, you have to have a big team." I have to admit, I wasn't necessarily in the dreaming mood. I didn't have goals back then, I didn't have a dream board; I didn't have a long-term vision for my life. I wasn't thinking about buying parcels of land, shopping at fine designer boutiques and traveling around the world. I was *surviving*. I wasn't *thriving*. I was surviving; and all of this talk about dreaming made me feel uncomfortable. The *only* thing I was focused on was paying my bills.

I hadn't heard this kind of stuff since I was in grammar school: "Follow your dreams". At first, I felt as if I was in the Twilight Zone or, better yet, Mr. Roger's neighborhood. These were adults talking about the dreams that they had in their hearts and how they achieved them. These were *very* successful individuals, that were living an incredible lifestyle, and I quickly figured out that they were probably on to something. If I wanted what they had, I had to do what they did. If I wanted change in my life, I had to make some changes.

I could no longer dwell in the past. I couldn't change the past, and the only one that keeps the past alive is us.

**The past only lives in our minds and, no matter how often we replay the scene, the ending is always the same.**

I also had to stop dwelling on the negatives in my current situation. If I focused on all the things that were wrong, I was destined to stay there, because you will get more of what you think about. No matter what you have gone through in the past, no matter how many setbacks you have suffered, no matter whom or what has tried to stop your progress, today is a new day!

I had to stop focusing on my current problems, and focus on the current possibilities.

To begin living an amazing life, I had to start looking at life through the eyes of faith and visualize the life that I wanted to live. *Never* let your past failures determine your future. Learn from them. Grow from them. You were born to win, you were born to break through barriers; you were created to be victorious.

> ***You were put on this earth to live a blessed, highly favored, abundant and giving life.***

Having a dream in your heart is what drives you to stop watching from the sidelines and play along. Dreams are goals. They are the targets that you strive for. They are the emotional juice that keeps you going when the going gets tough. Those with dreams and goals succeed for one simple reason: they know where they are going, they know what they want and they stay focused on it until they get there.

> ***So, what do YOU want?***
> ***What do you really want?***
> ***What does success mean to you?***

It is funny that when I ask people what they want, they are stunned, hesitant and at a loss for words: they simply don't know what to say. But if I ask you to list the things that you do not like about your current lifestyle or finances, you could build an incredible list. I don't like this. I despise this. This bothers me.

That fact alone is an indication that you are focusing on the negatives in your life. You are focusing on the wrong stuff, which is why it so easily pours out. We have a tendency to focus and think about the things that we don't want, or the things we don't like in our life.

The poet, Paul Valéry, wrote, "We hope vaguely, but dread precisely."

***Where you are today is a direct result of where your thoughts have brought you.***
***Where you will be tomorrow is a direct result of where your thoughts bring you.***

This is not a new fact. This philosophy is in the Bible, Proverbs 23:4 "As a man thinketh in his heart, so is he." Many books have been written about thinking and success. In the early 1900s, the legendary steel mogul, Andrew Carnegie, told Napoleon Hill, a young journalist, what he believed to be his "secret to success". Over the next 20 years, Hill interviewed over 500 wealthy and successful men, in order to gain their secrets. The results were his classic book *Think and Grow Rich.* "You become what you think about. What the mind of man can conceive, it will achieve." Best-selling author and minister Joel Osteen wrote in his book, *Your Best Life Now,* "If you dwell on positive thoughts, your life will move in that direction. If you continually think negative thoughts, you will live a negative life."

When I really understood this, I mean really *got* this, my life changed forever. I started to focus on my blessings instead of my misfortunes. I developed an attitude of gratitude. It is absolutely impossible to be in a bad mood if you start to think about how blessed you are. If we really sat down and started to count all of our blessings, we would be counting until the end of time. I wake up with a grateful heart. The more I focused on my blessings, the more blessings came my way. You WILL get what you think about.

It is simple: break the pattern, as I have, and all top achievers have. Nothing of greatness has ever been accomplished by a pessimist.

A friend of mine shared this very simple exercise with me and it really helped me fine-tune this in my own life.

The first thing you have to do is take a moment and write down all of the things you don't like about your current lifestyle or your current financial situation.

Go ahead: take a piece of paper, *right now*, and start making a list.

Now let's say you wrote down, "Not enough money", "Bills are piling up", "Just making ends meet", "Cant' afford the vacation that I want", "Don't see my spouse and children as much as I would like", "I don't have any free time", "I can't donate money the way I would like".

Now, obviously, by your list, these are the things that you DON'T want, these are the things that you DON'T like.

Now here is where the fun begins. Let's say, for instance, you have written down, "Not enough money".

Put a line through it ,and right next to it write down, "An abundance of money". If you wrote down, "I don't spend enough time with my children", put a line through that and write down, "I have quantity and quality time with my children". If you have written, "I don't have enough free time", put a line through that and write, "I have plenty of time to do the things that I love". *These* are the sentences that need to be focused on in order for you to achieve what they say. You can do this simple exercise in all areas of your life, your physical life, spiritual life, your relationships, everything.

The most important thing that you can do is to write these things down. The biggest mistake that people make is not getting this down on paper. You may have thought about your dreams and goals, but if they are not written down, I can guarantee that you are not getting what you desire. If you don't write this stuff down, all you have are *intentions* that are simply seeds without any soil. The more you write down, the better. The more that is written down, the clearer the vision becomes.

At the writing of this book, this is my current mission statement. The first paragraph I have taken from portions of a newsletter I received from Joel Osteen. I found the words to be inspirational and powerful.

*I am Blessed and highly favored. I am blessed with God's divine purpose and perfect plan for my life. I am blessed with gifts, God-given abilities and guidance. I am blessed with strength of character, self-determination and self-*

*control. I am blessed with family and friends, faith and freedom. I am blessed with health, happiness, favor and fulfillment. I am blessed with promotion, protection, prosperity and provision. I am blessed with a spirit of obedience, supernatural success and a positive attitude. I am blessed with a fresh start and a new outlook on life. I am looking forward to the new thing God will do in my life today.*

*I am thankful for the life that Matt and I have built together, we become closer each day and continually show our love and respect for each other. Our life is filled with wonderful first time experiences and adventures.*

*I have an open, fun and loving relationship with Sabrina and Monica. I am thankful for the inspirational guidance that I receive each day, may I use this to help guide them. We create happy memories together.*

*I choose to be a life giver and give love freely to others. I am a good and loyal friend. I am a loving and helpful daughter.*

*I have a healthy and physically fit body*

*Matt and I have a tremendous and positive influence on all of those that we are in business with. We serve our team so that we may lead. We have a mutual respect for all of our fellow leaders, peace and harmony.*

*Money comes to us easily, frequently and abundantly.
Our income continues to grow substantially each year
and our giving continues to grow substantially each year.*

*We are living the life of our dreams.*

*We have inspired millions of people to believe in their
greatness and achieve success.*

My personal mission statement has changed and
evolved over the years and it will continue to change and
evolve as my life continues to change and evolve. When I
read it I get emotionally charged, because it's mine.

What is *yours* going to look like? What are *you*
going to speak into your life each day? Will you choose to
speak words of life or words of death?

If you don't like what you are getting, change.
Change your thoughts, change your life. Change your
words, change your life. Change your focus, change your
life.

**You have the power to think thoughts of life or death.
You have the power to speak words of life or death.
Choose life, choose love, and choose happiness,
prosperity and abundance.**

# Chapter 7

# The Dream, The Journey, The Prize

**How does a small rope tied around the ankle of a 4,000-pound elephant keep that elephant in its place?** Obviously the elephant has the strength and the power to break free, but it doesn't. Why? The elephant has been conditioned to stay in its place. When an elephant is young, it is secured by one of its ankles by a steel chain. Every time the animal tries to break loose, it is jerked back. Eventually its ankle becomes raw and sore. The elephant will associate becoming free with pain. *They no longer try.* Then all it takes is a small rope to constrain this massive animal.

We are often conditioned in the same way. As we start to build our network marketing business, we experience some pain. Maybe it is a negative neighbor or friend who decides this isn't for them. Because we associate a "no" with pain, we no longer want to experience the pain. *We stop attempting to break free.* We stay in the same place, with the same job, with the same income and the same lifestyle. The very thing that was making us uncomfortable has now become temporarily comfortable.

This comfort zone is only there for a very short while and will lead to a life of discomfort. I realized that if I got a little *uncomfortable* in the beginning, I could be *comfortable* the rest of my life. *If I stayed in my comfort zone now, I would be uncomfortable for the rest of my life.*

There are three words that describe the journey of any successful achievement. It is the DREAM, the JOURNEY and the PRIZE. The first essential part of the formula is the dream.

I was encouraged to dream again, through this process, I learned amazing, life-altering things. Having *any* kind of dream is good. It brings many benefits to your life. It will give you more interest in each day. It will give you a stronger sense of purpose and direction and a keener understanding of this gift of life. You will also have more personal motivation to take action and make that dream come true. The bigger the dream the better, simply because big dreams are more exciting than small ones, Victor Hugo wrote, "Dream no small dreams for they have not the power to stir the soul."

**A big dream is REALLY what you want and, more importantly, that dream that has been stuffed inside of you is quite possibly what you are here on earth to achieve.**

Are you doing anything about your dream? Did you do anything yesterday, or have you done anything today, to move you closer to your dream? Do you plan to take any specific action tomorrow or during the week? Do you think about it each and every day and plan on what you can do to make it a reality?

If you are not fired up about your dream and it is not in the forefront on a day-to-day basis, there is little chance that you will make it come to fruition. We tend to put things on the back-burner and we keep putting them off. Another day goes by, another week, another year, and we are not any closer than we were when we first started thinking about our dreams again in the first place. I am truly convinced that keeping a dream alive in your heart *and* mind will make your life more rewarding, wondrous, and exciting.

So often we get so caught up in the challenges of the moment, focusing on the wrong things, that we forget the prize that is awaiting us. We want the dream, but we also want to skip the struggle that is an essential part of the journey, and go right to the prize. It cannot and will not happen that way.

Have you ever heard of an Olympian dreaming of the gold medal, then just showing up and stepping onto the podium? The athlete has to be committed and dedicated to go through years of vigorous training, muscle soreness, emotional ups and downs and lost competitions. They choose not to focus on the hardship of the journey; they learn to embrace the journey and enjoy the process because they know that it is going to lead them to the prize, the gold.

How often do we get so caught up in the task at hand that we forget why we are there in the first place? At the first sign of adversity, we want to throw in the towel and call it a day.

I experienced this phenomenon first hand. I was pregnant for the first time. I was thrilled. I do, however, think that there is some secret society of moms that choose not to share the whole childbirth experience with newly pregnant moms-to-be. I would ask, "So, what is it like?" and mothers would just smile and say, "It is fine, when you see the baby; you don't remember any of it."

I signed up for a child birth class. The instructor was a complete throwback from the 60s. She would have fit right in with the flower-child movement, and believed that childbirth was natural and drugs should not interfere with this beautiful process. I am woman, hear me roar! I bought in to her philosophy, especially when she told us in the class that we could simply *breathe* through the pain. This was an entirely new concept for me. I never realized that we could breathe through pain! Breathing through the pain sounded so wonderful! Now that I look back, wanting to have natural childbirth is kind of like wanting to have natural dentistry. I mean, we *do* have the technology.

When the day arrived and the contractions started, I went straight to the hospital. I had booked a birthing suite: it had a hot tub, a sitting area and a big screen T.V. I thought the whole process was going to be so easy, a piece of cake, and I was going to be *breathing* through all of the pain. I had visions of entertaining family and friends in the birthing suite once the baby arrived.

Fast forward a few hours. Well, the breathing thing wasn't working as I thought it would. It got painful, very painful. I was huffing, puffing, wincing and whining. I finally yelled, ok, I screamed for the nurse. (I take no responsibility for my behavior during this time.)

In through the door, there she stood, in the flesh, Nurse Ratched. No, it really wasn't her, but she sure did act like her. "What do you need?" she asked with perched lips and narrow eyes. I then shouted, "I am in a lot of pain! I am very uncomfortable!" She then smugly asked, "Well, have you tried breathing?" "What?!!! Breathe? Breathe? You breathe!" At the sounds of what was happening in my room, my doctor happened to be down the hall, or maybe he was on another floor. Anyway, he heard me and came to my room.

"Johnna, calm down, what is going on?" he asked in a calm voice. I then said, "Doctor, I don't feel like doing this right now! I would like to go home and come back tomorrow!" He laughed and said, "Johnna, you are going to have a beautiful baby in your arms, you have to get through this, to get to that. Focus on your child." In that moment, be brought me back to my reason. I was so over-focused on the pain, I forgot *why* I was there. I was ready to skip out on the birth of my own daughter! When the moment arrived, and she was born, I held her in my arms. It was one of the most incredible moments of my life.

I understand that hearing the word "NO" is uncomfortable. It doesn't feel good. I received a very significant "no" in the early stages of building my network marketing business.

I shared the business with a neighbor. I believed him to be perfect for the business. That was mistake number 1. We start thinking, "If I could just get Jerry! Jerry is going to be the one! Jerry is going to tear this business up!" I shared some information over the phone, and he agreed to attend a meeting with me. He sat in the front row, arms crossed with a scowl on his face. Not the positive body language that I was expecting. After the meeting was over, not only did he say "no", he wanted to tell me why I shouldn't do it either. He went on and on about how these types of companies don't ever last and how this will never work. Because I was young in the business, and my own personal belief wasn't as high as it should have been, I actually believed him. I put my worth in the hands of someone else.

I called Matt, who was not my husband at this time; he was my up-line leader in the business. I told him that I was thinking that I should call the corporate recruiting firm that I used to work for and get a job. I told him all of the things that Jerry told me, repeating all of the negativity that was shared with me. Matt stopped me and said, "Johnna, that is fine, but have you figured out who is going to be with your daughters 10 hours a day, while you are at work?" Like my doctor did years earlier, Matt brought me back to my "why"; he brought me back to my reason for building the business in the first place.

I went home that evening, and had a very restless night of sleep. I woke up in the middle of the night and thought, "Who does Jerry think he is? If Jerry was such a financial genius, if Jerry was a guru when it came to making money, Jerry would not be my neighbor!" I then got a total resolve to prove him wrong.

I could have let the pain of the "no" take me out of the game. I chose to go after my dream, and those that wanted to come along, could come along, and those that didn't, didn't'.

Years later, after Matt and I had married, we were enjoying an incredible vacation on the island of Utila, a small island off of the coast of Honduras. We were scuba diving and searching for whale shark. The water is incredibly clear and the bluest blue that you can imagine. It is paradise. As we were heading off to another dive sight, we came across a pod of dolphin. There were at least 10 of them swimming in the wild and following our boat. The captain of the boat said, "OK, here is your chance to swim with dolphin in the wild. Grab your mask, fins and snorkel and jump in." I jumped in the water and just floated at the surface looking through the water with my mask. There they were, dolphin spinning up and down, going to the surface, then diving down deep. They swam around us, and played. It was an astounding display of gentle beauty. As I floated, experiencing this once in a lifetime experience, in this incredibly beautiful place; I thought to myself, "I am so thankful I never quit. I am so thankful I chose to follow my dream." Then I thought, "Gee, I wonder what Jerry is doing today?"

The world is full of critics. If you want to be a great leader and accomplish great things you will have to live with the comments and the actions of people who want to bring you down. One of the things that I have discovered is that not everyone is going to be happy for your success and prosperity, or your pursuit of those things

After studying leadership, and the most influential leaders in history, I quickly understood that every person who has done great things, those that have changed the world, all had critics. The finger pointer who said, "You are not doing it right!"

Instead of letting criticism bring you down, you have to take it as a challenge and get stronger from it, build on it. Always keep your motives pure and your purpose and your goals in front of you. Don't be swayed by what others say.

## Hope, opportunity and the American Dream

The future is bright; in fact, it is the brightest it has ever been. In order for us to look into the future, it is important for us to understand our past, and to not take our past and what lies ahead in our future for granted. The United States of America is a country that was built on dreams. Our ancestors chose to take the risk of putting their lives on the line and fight for freedom. Freedom to them; was worth any price and any struggle.

So, what is the American Dream? James Truslow Adams was the first to coin the phrase, he said, "The American Dream is that dream of a land in which life should be better and richer and fuller for everyone, with opportunity for each according to ability and achievement." This "dream" of America spread across the world, which caused masses of people to come to this country in pursuit of life, liberty and happiness in the land of opportunity. I believe that we live in the greatest country in the world. Let's not forget for a moment that people are not crossing our borders in masses in order to leave.

One of the strongest attractions of living in the United States of America is that there is no limit to the height and scope of your dream. Ellis Island was the launching pad for many. Immigrants from Ireland, Italy, Russia, Germany, Spain, England, France, Sweden, Australia and many other nations knew that once they passed through Ellis Island, a new life was theirs.

The basic freedom to dream what you will is one of the things that make this country so great. "Only in America" people around the world still say, "can big dreams come true." People fought and died just for the chance to reach America's shores.

My great grandparents left an impoverished Italy for the same reasons: to come to the land of the free, to be a part of a country where the sky was the limit, to be able to go as far as you want to go, and become whatever you want to be. I can venture to say, that many of you have ancestors in your family tree that have done the same thing. They came over on ships in horrible conditions, in pursuit of a dream. Their struggle paved the way so that future generations could have a better life. How often do we take it for granted?

My great grandparents did not speak English. They felt it an honor to learn the language. They wanted the ability to communicate with their fellow Americans. I have often thought of what would happen if all of the immigrants that make up the "melting pot" decided to hold true to their native tongue. Studies have shown that we would have over 40 different languages spoken in our country. The United States of America would have become the Divided States of America. How can you possibly be united if you can't communicate with one another? My great grandparents were proud to raise their right hands and become American citizens, speaking English in the process.

Many have dreamt and struggled and led the way for all of us. Andrew Carnegie immigrated to America as a teen. He built up the world's largest steel mills and became one of the richest men in the world. He gave it all away and helped build our country's libraries. Thomas Edison struggled through 10,000 attempts on inventing the light bulb. Franklin Delano Roosevelt, a man who could no longer walk, brought the world's aggressors to their knees.

## Enthusiasm

All of those that have achieved anything of significance had the dream, experienced the journey and achieved their prize. The key is how you handle the ups and downs of the journey. When you remain true to your purpose and your dream, the "struggle" becomes an important part of your growth and understanding. When you add enthusiasm to the process, there is a deep enjoyment in the journey. Even when things don't go as planned, or when there is disappointment. You will be like an arrow that is moving toward a target. The key is to simply "enjoy the process".The only time that there is stress in the process is when you want to arrive at the goal *more* than you want to be doing what you are doing. People do not want to get in business with people that are stressed out. Stress will always diminish your quality and effectiveness. Ralph Waldo Emerson said that, "Nothing great has ever been achieved without enthusiasm." The actual word "enthusiasm" comes from an ancient Greek – *en* and *theos*, meaning God within. When you tap into your enthusiasm, you will not be doing the business alone. Enjoyment of what you are doing, combined with a goal or vision of what you are working toward, *becomes* enthusiasm.

My truest enthusiasm in building the business did not stem from what I could get from it. My deepest enthusiasm will always come from how the business can serve and enrich others.

In the pursuit of your dream, you will certainly be in good company. You will be one of those whose lives are enriched. When you reach the realization and fulfillment of your dream, you will know that you have *truly lived*, perhaps more vibrantly than a great majority of the people in the world.

*You will always remember the joy of that day, that moment, when you saw your dream become a reality. YOU will be able to say with all the other dreamers who found fulfillment, "It was a dream come true."*

# Chapter 8

# You Have a
# Decision to Make

According to *Webster's New World Dictionary*, the word "decide" means to bring an end to a vacillation, doubt or dispute, etc. by making up one's mind as to an action, course or judgment; finality in a decision, resolve implies firmness of intention to carry through a decision.

When I was about 8 years old, my parents took my brother and me to Disneyworld. We drove from Chicago. My brother and I piled up in the back seat with our books and toys, anything to keep us occupied. Within the first hour the question was out, "How much longer? How many more minutes?"

Many who enter network marketing want to ask others that very same question. "How long will it take me to become successful?" No one can answer that question because *you* have the answer.

## You decide when, how long and how fast

Our lives are made up decisions and choices. My life is positive and full of joy because that is what I choose. I have decided how I am going to live and be.

It wasn't always like that for me. The person I am today is a world apart from the person who entered the world of network marketing over a decade ago. I was negative and I felt like a failure. My marriage was dissolved, my children were going to be in daycare, and I was in major debt. If I had goals or a dream board back then, none of these things would have been on it.

I started to work on *me*, on *my* attitude and *my* belief system. Matt had given me a book called *Awaken the Giant Within* by Anthony Robbins. The concepts of this book knocked me upside my head. It made me wake up and take control of my life. I started to realize that where I was at that time in my life was a direct result of every decision I made up to that point. Not just the big decisions, the little day-in and day-out decisions. Where I was physically, emotionally, spiritually, in my relationships, and where I was financially were a direct result of *my* decisions.

It would have been very easy to play the victim; which is why so many people do. It would have been easy to cast blame, blaming other people or circumstances. It's this person's fault, or the economy's fault. I had to stop blaming and feeling sorry for myself and take full responsibility for where I was in my life. Was it easy? No. What is necessary? Yes.

I had to realize that this was my doing; all of it. This was *my* responsibility. This was *my* fault. This is *my* life. I am the star of my show. You are the star of your show and everyone around you are simply extras.

I had to take responsibility for all of the decisions I had made up to that point of my life. I had to feel the weight of it. Initially it did not feel very good. Initially it was painful to come to this realization. But, when I sorted it all out, the weight lifted. It was amazing.

***In a single, life-altering moment, I realized that if the decisions I had made up to this point got me to where I am at, that means that every decision that I make from this point forward could literally alter my future.***

I could shape my own destiny. I decided from that moment on to make my life a masterpiece and become who I was meant to be.

Ask yourself, "How am I going to live today to shape the tomorrow that I want?" Who will you become in the next 10 years? Where will you be? How will you live? What will you contribute to the lives of others?

If you don't make decisions about how you are going to live tomorrow, then I guess you have already made a decision. My whole life changed in an instant the day I decided who and what I was committed to *having* and *being* in my life – the day I realized that my future was shaped by my own decisions and actions.

Two distinctive types of decisions are decisions of *convenience* and decisions of *commitment*. A decision of convenience seems like a good idea at the time. It feels right and is easy. The decisions of convenience produce little or nothing. What feels good today, as you begin any type of change in your life, will at one time or another no longer feel easy or convenient, so we stop doing it.

The second and most impactful type of decision is a decision to commit. These types of decisions produce results and permanent change. It is a decision that has long-term thinking attached to it. It has resolve and zero tolerance. There is no turning back. A true commitment is a decision to do something, to be something, no matter the obstacles; no matter whether you feel like it tomorrow or the next day, no matter what results you are currently experiencing.

Sometimes people have difficulty making any type of commitment to anything. They spend their whole lives jumping from one thing to the next. They are constantly looking for a quick and easy way to success: when they don't find it, they jump to something else. I don't believe for a minute that you just have one chance to do something incredible with your life. But, I am not naïve enough to believe that we have an unlimited amount of chances either.

Sooner or later you have to settle in and say, "This is a great opportunity, this is a good company, and I am going to take it all the way. I am going to take my business to the top."

The saddest thing that we see in the business is when someone with great potential and great talent gives up before they've given themselves a chance to win. It isn't sad because they have given up on their business, it is sad because they have given up on themselves. They then go back to settling for something less than their dreams. Things often look worse before they start to turn around. People often give up at the worst moment: if they would have just stuck it out, and sucked it up, they would begin to see their efforts pay off. Unfortunately, quitters become good losers. If you quit once, it is easier each and every time you quit. You can then quit again and again and again.

*When quitting is no longer an option, it is amazing how you learn to take any challenge and turn them into opportunities to grow, instead of using them as an excuse to fail.*

Making committed decisions is something that you should help build and encourage in your team. Your personal commitment is passed on to your people. If your commitment is weak or strong, that is what is passed on.

When you finally decide to commit and make a total commitment, nothing in your life will be the same. Maybe for the first time there will be some direction and purpose. Making a total commitment will help *you* develop a mental toughness and this will help develop a mental toughness in the members of your team.

## Candy Land

Matt and I were only married about a year when the girls, our daughters Sabrina and Monica, wanted to play the board game *Candy Land* with him. Sabrina was 6 years old and Monica was 4. Sabrina was only a few squares away from King Candy and the Candy Castle. She was very excited and could taste victory. She drew a card and was sent back all the way to Gooey Gum Drop Land. She threw up her arms and exclaimed, "I quit!" Matt looked at her and asked, "You what?" She is now perturbed and crying, "I quit! I will never win now!" Matt then asked, "Sabrina, are you a winner or a whiner?" She wailed, "I'm a winnerrrrrrrrr, who's gonna loooooooose!" He then said, "Sabrina, quitters never win and winners never quit. If you quit now, you will stop any chance of winning, you have to stay in the game in order to win." She reluctantly put her gingerbread man back on the board.

A few turns later, Monica won the game. Now, you know that 4 year olds are very gracious winners. She started to dance around in her victory. With that, Sabrina went into hysterics, "I told you I was going to lose!! I told you I was going to lose!" Matt then said, "Sabrina, now calm down honey, you have to understand that success is never certain, and failure is never final." With that, she scrunched up her face and said, "Huh?" Matt then remembered he was talking to a 6-year-old. "Sabrina, you may have lost this game, but you can play again." She then asked, "But, what if I lose again?" He said, "You just play again." That day, Sabrina played *until she won.*

## Faith and belief

You have to decide to act in faith and belief. It all starts with faith. It all starts with belief. Do you really want a free life? Do you really want an incredible lifestyle? Do you really want to make a difference in the lives of others? Do you want to be respected and admired? *You* have to have faith. Faith in your company, faith in the leadership, faith in your products or services: faith itself produces confident behavior.

Feed the faith and it will grow. Feed the fear and it will grow. If you continually feed your faith, you will starve the fear out.

*Feeding the faith begins with TAKING ACTION in the decisions that you make.*

Sticking with those decisions and following through on those decisions is a powerful process.

I often ask people if they would trust someone who lied to them over and over again. The answer is always "no". How can we trust, believe and have faith in ourselves if we keep lying to ourselves. We say that we are going to do something, and that we have *decided*, yet something gets uncomfortable and we don't follow through. This act alone hurts our own self-belief. Breaking the pattern is simple: just make the decision, and *follow through* on that decision.

This is no different to when any new business starts. All are founded on hope and faith. When there is no faith in the beginning, there is no hope of ever winning.

How do you show faith? How do you show belief? I heard a story once about a Baptist church down south. They didn't have rain in the county for several months. They decided to have a prayer meeting to pray for rain. When the time came for the meeting to begin, Brother John was absent. He was their leader and he was nowhere to be found. They looked out the window, and there was Brother John walking down the sidewalk toward the church on a bright sunny day, with his umbrella up.

### How do we show belief?

In order for you to be a hero for your team and your people, in order to be someone who walks in faith and demonstrates belief to your group, you have to do things that teach them to believe.

What are you doing? What have you done today? What have you done yesterday that demonstrated to your team and your prospects that *you believe* more than they do?

As the leader, I believe that I have to do more, I have to believe more, I have to show more, I have to read more, I have to be more energetic, I have to be more positive. I have to have a bigger dream than those that I lead. Big dreamers inspire others to dream big. Share your dream and your vision with your team every chance you get. The size of your dream will determine the amount of time and energy that you are willing to contribute.

***Make the decision to have a superior attitude.***
***Anyone can be up when they are up.***
***A leader is up when they are down.***

Leaders fuel themselves continually with pure positive thoughts and act in an upbeat manner at all times, not just when they feel like it.

We admire and respect the majestic eagle. There are many lessons in nature, and the story of the mother eagle and her young is no exception.

The mother eagle stirs the nest. When it is time for the young eaglets to fly, the mother eagle goes into the nest and tears out all the soft down that held her young. She will expose the briar and the thorns, making her young uncomfortable. They move from inside the nest to the edge of the nest. The mother eagle will then take her wing tip and gently flip the eaglet off of the edge. As it is tumbling down in mid air, if it doesn't flap its wings, she will catch the eaglet with her powerful talons and fly up as high as she can fly. She will then let go again and again and again, until the eaglet stretches its wings and flies, and soars across the sky.

Have you made the *decision* to fly? Have you made the *decision* to soar? Have you made the *decision* to design the rest of your life, starting today?

# Chapter 9

# A Daily Dose of Inspiration

I believe in the importance of being inspired on a daily basis. Good inspiration will enhance your intellect and move your emotions in a positive direction. Much of this inspiration comes from those that have achieved greatness in their life. It allows me to hear their words, get inside their heads and glean some wisdom. These are some of my favorites.

*"Do unto others as you would have them do unto you."*

Jesus

*"A leader of one may someday be a leader of many, but if you can't lead one (yourself), you will never lead any."*

Matt Parr

*"Don't work for money, work for success, and the money will chase you down."*

Dick Loehr

*"Life is either a daring adventure or nothing at all."*

Helen Keller

*"A great attitude does much more than turn on the lights in our worlds; it seems to magically connect us to all sorts of serendipitous opportunities that were somehow absent before the change."*

Dale Carnegie

*"I will do today what other won't, so that tomorrow I may live the way they can't."*

Anonymous

*"Success is not final, failure is not fatal: it is the courage to continue that counts."*

Winston Churchill

*"Success is how high you bounce when you hit bottom."*

George S. Patton

*"It is what you learn after you know it all that counts."*

John Wooden

*"Are you green and growing or ripe and rotting?"*

Ray Kroc

*"There are two ways to live your life. One as though nothing were a miracle. The other as though everything is a miracle."*

Albert Einstein

*"Whatever is true, noble, right, pure, lovely, and admirable; if anything is excellent or praiseworthy-think about such things."*

Phil 4:8

*"If we don't change our direction, we are likely to end up where we are headed."*

Chinese Proverb

*"Far better to dare mighty things, win glorious triumphs, even though checkered by failure, than to rank with those poor spirits who neither enjoy much nor suffer much, because they live in the gray twilight that knows no victory nor defeat."*

Theodore Roosevelt

*"The ultimate measure of a man is not where he stands in moments of comfort and convenience, but where he stands at times of challenge and controversy."*

Martin Luther King Jr.

*"As a man thinketh in his heart so is he."*

Proverbs 23:4

*"If you can dream it, you can do it."*

Walt Disney

*"Inaction breeds doubt and fear. Action breeds confidence and courage. If you want to conquer fear, do not sit home and think about it. Go out and get busy."*

Dale Carnegie

*"This too shall pass"*

Solomon

*"We are what we think. All that we are arises with our thoughts. With our thoughts, we make our world."*

Buddha

*"As we look ahead into the next century, the greatest leaders will be those who empower others."*

Bill Gates

*"If you dwell on positive thoughts, your life will move in that direction. If you continually think negative thoughts, you will live a negative life."*

Joel Osteen

*"There is little difference between those who cannot read and those who will not read – the result of both is ignorance."*

Jim Rohn

*"Our greatest glory is not in never falling but in rising every time we fall."*

Confucius

*"Man's finest hour is the moment when he has worked his heart out in a good cause and lies exhausted on the field of battle, victorious."*

Vince Lombardi

*"Go confidently in the direction of your dreams. Live the life you have imagined."*

Henry David Thorough

*"No one can make you feel inferior without your consent."*

Eleanor Roosevelt

*"We are what we repeatedly do. Excellence, therefore, is not an act but a habit."*

Aristotle

*"Don't wish for it to be easier, wish for you to be better."*

Jim Rohn

*"What the mind of man can conceive, it can achieve."*

Napoleon Hill

*"10% of life happens, 90% is how we react to it."*

Charles Schwab

*"Live as if you were to die tomorrow; Learn as if you were to live forever."*

Mahatma Gandhi

*"If you think you can or think you can't, you are right."*

Henry Ford

*"America is too great for small dreams."*

Ronald Reagan

*"One man cannot hold another man down in the ditch without remaining down in the ditch with him."*

Booker T. Washington

*"We teach what we know, we reproduce what we are."*

John Maxwell

*"Nothing can stop a man with the right mental attitude from achieving his goal; nothing can help the man with the wrong mental attitude."*

Thomas Jefferson

*"If we all did the things we are capable of, we would astound ourselves."*

Thomas Edison

*"Let no one ever come to you without leaving happier."*

Mother Theresa

*"Any fool can criticize, condemn, and complain – and most do."*

Dale Carnegie

# Closing Letter

There comes a time in your life when you realize that if you stand still, you will remain at that point forever.

You realize that if you fall and stay down, life will pass you by.

Life's circumstances are not always what you might wish them to be. The pattern of life does not necessarily go as you plan.

Beyond any understanding, you may at times be led in a direction that you never imagined, dreamed or designed.

Shake off your "what ifs" and tear up the excuses.

Whatever *was* is in the past. Whatever *is* is what is important. The past is a brief reflection that only lives in our minds. The future is yet to be realized.

*Today is here.*

Take action with courage, faith, determination.

Keep your belief in yourself and walk into your new journey with confidence.

Soon your path will become the most comfortable and most rewarding you could have ever hoped to follow.

*God gave us this gift of life,*
*what we do with it is our gift to God.*

You may contact Johnna Parr at:

johnna@mjparr.com

Or

Visit the website:

www.whenthedreamisbigenough.com